MUCH SOUND AND FURY, OR THE NEW JIM CROW?

MUCH SOUND AND FURY, OR THE NEW JIM CROW?

The Twenty-First Century's Restrictive New Voting Laws and Their Impact

Edited by
Michael A. Smith

Published by State University of New York Press, Albany

© 2022 State University of New York

All rights reserved

Printed in the United States of America

No part of this book may be used or reproduced in any manner whatsoever without written permission. No part of this book may be stored in a retrieval system or transmitted in any form or by any means including electronic, electrostatic, magnetic tape, mechanical, photocopying, recording, or otherwise without the prior permission in writing of the publisher.

For information, contact State University of New York Press, Albany, NY
www.sunypress.edu

Library of Congress Cataloging-in-Publication Data

Name: Smith, Michael A., 1970– editor.
Title: Much sound and fury, or the new Jim Crow? : the twenty-first century's restrictive new voting laws and their impact / [edited by] Michael A. Smith.
Description: Albany : State University of New York Press, [2022] | Includes bibliographical references and index.
Identifiers: LCCN 2021040887 (print) | LCCN 2021040888 (ebook) | ISBN 9781438486833 (hardcover : alk. paper) | ISBN 9781438486826 (pbk. : alk. paper) | ISBN 9781438486840 (ebook)
Subjects: LCSH: African Americans—Suffrage—History. | African Americans—Civil rights—History. | African Americans—Suffrage—Mississippi—History. | Suffrage—United States—States—History. | Voter registration—United States—History. | Voter suppression—United States—History. | Gerrymandering—United States—History.
Classification: LCC KF4893 .M83 2022 (print) | LCC KF4893 (ebook) | DDC 342.73/072—dc23/eng/20211004
LC record available at https://lccn.loc.gov/2021040887
LC ebook record available at https://lccn.loc.gov/2021040888

10 9 8 7 6 5 4 3 2 1

Contents

List of Illustrations   vii

Chapter 1
Introduction   1
    Michael A. Smith and Chapman Rackaway

Chapter 2
Black Voting Rights 1865–2016: Two Reconstructions and
Four Mississippi Plans   9
    Russell Brooker

Chapter 3
The Impact of Voter ID Laws on County Turnout in the
2016 Presidential Election   45
    Ryan E. Voris

Chapter 4
Backlash! Do Restrictive Voting Laws Mobilize Their Opponents?   71
    Michael A. Smith

Chapter 5
Using Cross-Sectional, Time Series, and Border Analysis to
Identify the Impact of Restrictive Voting Laws   87
    Bekah Selby and Michael A. Smith

Chapter 6
Contemporary Effects of Felony Disenfranchisement upon
Election Turnout and Partisan Vote Share   109
    Linda M. Trautman and Bekah Selby

Chapter 7
Using Mathematics to Understand How Gerrymandering
Affects Partisan Voting Power   125
   Brian Hollenbeck and Deborah G. Hann

Chapter 8
Civil Rights Groups Respond   143
   Kevin Anderson

Conclusion   159
   Michael A. Smith and Chapman Rackaway

Afterword on the 2020 Election   165
   Michael A. Smith

Contributors   175

Index   179

Illustrations

Tables

2.1	Two Reconstructions and Four Mississippi Plans	11
2.2	Voter Registration in Seven Southern States before and after the Voting Rights Act in Percent	27
2.3	Number of Black Elected Officials in Seven Southern States after the Voting Rights Act	27
3.1	State Voter ID Requirement and County Turnout in 2016	59
4.1	Dependent Variable: Whether or Not the Respondent Voted	78
4.2	Dependent Variable: Whether the Respondent Voted for Obama	81
5.1	Effect of Independent Variables on Republican Share of Vote	95
5.2	Effect of Independent Variables on Democratic Share of Vote	96
5.3	Effect of Independent Variables on Independent/3rd Party Share of Vote	97
5.4	Effect of Independent Variables on Turnout	98
5.5	Effect of Independent Variables on Republican Share of Vote (Focus Only on One Law)	99
5.6	Effect of Independent Variables on Democratic Share of Vote (Focus Only on One Law)	100

viii | Illustrations

5.7	Effect of Independent Variables on Independent/3rd Party Share of Vote (Focus Only on One Law)	101
5.8	Effect of Independent Variables on Turnout (Focus Only on One Law)	102
5.9	Effect of Independent Variables on Turnout and Party over Time	103
5.10	Effect of Independent Variables on Turnout and Party with Interaction Effects	105
6.1	Aggregate and Black Disenfranchisement (Percentage of the VAP) by Region, 2016	115
6.2	State Fixed Regression of the Effects of Felony Disenfranchisement upon Turnout	118
7.1	Compactness Scores for "Lyon" Map in Figure 7.3	130
7.2	Compactness Scores for "Lyon" Map in Figure 7.4	130
7.3	Wasted Votes in Districts in Figure 7.6	132
7.4	Efficiency Gaps of Hypothetical Districts	133
7.5	Number of Votes out of 100 for Party X	135
7.6	Seats Won by X in 52:48 Distribution with 100, 1,000, and 10,000 Voters	135
7.7	Results of 1,000 Districting Simulations for Iowa, 2016	139
7.8	Results of 3,000 Hypothetical Maps for North Carolina, 2016	139
A.1	State Adjustments to the Coronavirus Pandemic 2020	167

Figures

3.1	ID Laws in U.S. States, 2016.	53
3.2	Predicted County Turnout.	61
3.3	Estimated Differences in County Turnout.	62
7.1	Hypothetical Distribution of 100 Voters in "Lyon."	126

7.2	First Hypothetical Four-District Map for "Lyon."	127
7.3	Second Hypothetical Four-District Map for "Lyon."	128
7.4	Third Hypothetical Four-District Map for "Lyon."	128
7.5	Hypothetical 52:48 Distribution of 100 Voters.	131
7.6	Map of 52:48 Distribution with Packing and Cracking.	132
7.7	Compact Districts in 52:48 District.	133
7.8	Low Efficiency Gap Districts in 52:48 District.	134
7.9a	Iowa Map With 3–1 Democratic Advantage, 2016.	137
7.9b	Iowa Map With 2–2 Split, 2016.	137
7.9c	Iowa Map With 3–1 Republican Advantage, 2016.	138
7.9d	Iowa Map With 4–0 Republican Advantage, 2016.	138

Chapter 1

Introduction

Michael A. Smith and Chapman Rackaway

Proof of Citizenship in the Unlikeliest of Places

It is not unusual to hear about the Bible in American politics, but in the twenty-first century, it is not usually used as a form of identification. For Jo French and Evelyn Howard, the Bible was used for just that purpose. French, who was born in Arkansas and later moved to Kansas, was unable to get a copy of her birth certificate from Arkansas and had to use a note of her birth in a family Bible to prove her citizenship in 2016 so she could legally vote in Kansas. In 2014, just two years prior, 92-year-old Evelyn Howard presented a Bible to her state's chief elections official. Despite having already voted in eighteen presidential elections, Howard was put in a difficult position as she prepared to register and vote, having moved from Minnesota to Kansas in 2013. The family Bible was the only record of Howard's birth, and the secretary of state deemed the informal record adequate documentation to allow Howard to vote.

The use of a Bible to prove citizenship by birth was not the only thing Howard and French had in common. They both moved to the state that is in the center of a roiling contemporary controversy over the right to vote. Kansas had become a national touchstone over voting rights, primarily because of the emergence of a single figure: Kris Kobach, an anti–illegal immigration activist who served as Kansas secretary of state from 2011–19. Kobach served as the author and architect of a policy agenda that signaled a significant shift, advising state and election officials in other states while simultaneously spearheading the effort in Kansas. For more than a half-century, reforms at the federal and state levels have focused on the expansion of the voting franchise, but from 2003–2016, state-level reforms concentrated on restriction of the franchise, particularly in Republican-voting states.

Plan of Book

After a brief introduction, this book begins with an in-depth consideration of the history of voting rights in the United States, starting shortly before the Civil War and continuing through the present day. The discussion shows how the arc of this story includes two periods of reconstruction—the time period and associated policies formally known as Reconstruction, immediately following the Civil War, and a second period of reconstruction that consisted of civil rights activism, court rulings, and constitutional amendments that occurred primarily during the mid-to-late twentieth century, reaching its zenith with the passage of the Voting Rights Act in 1965.

The two periods of reconstruction included a host of changes intended to expand the franchise for people of color—African Americans in particular. Not only did African American former slaves and their descendants gain the right to vote, but many who participated in the confederacy, including hundreds of thousands of Confederate States of America (CSA) veterans, were stripped of their own voting rights due to their role in the "rebellion." Numerous African American officials were elected to public office by a dramatically changed electorate after the ratification of the Fifteenth Amendment in 1870. The end of Reconstruction and the resurgence of states' rights brought all of this to an abrupt halt, with numerous chicaneries such as the grandfather clause, the poll tax, literacy tests, and egregiously gerrymandered districts. All of this began before the election of 1876, but accelerated dramatically afterward, due to the political compromises that Republicans made with the South to end the electoral deadlock of that year's presidential election. The chapter's author calls this backlash the first of four Mississippi Plans—reactionary policies meant to roll back gains in voting rights. During the Second Mississippi plan, beginning in 1889, violence and fear were added to the other measures as a way of denying African Americans access to the ballot box. The Ku Klux Klan, which grew rapidly during this era and reached its membership peak in the 1920s, joined other terror groups in using lynching—often threatened, sometimes carried out—to intimidate their targets away from voting. During this period, the federal government and courts frequently turned a blind eye, while some state governments, particularly in the South, actually encouraged the practice, with the white "Citizens' Councils" of Mississippi being a particularly stark example.

The Third Mississippi Plan was a reaction to the second reconstruction era, and it began in the 1970s. The author argues that this era saw yet more attempts to weaken the votes of African Americans, though the means of doing so became more subtle. Methods included at-large elections and multimember districts using winner-take-all voting, which both had the effect of preventing the creation of many minority-majority districts, which in turn may have elected people of color to office. This era was something of a mixed bag for voting rights. It included the Voting Rights Act Amendments of 1992, which called for the drawing of more majority-minority districts. It also included the National Voter Registration Act of 1996 (NVRA), popularly known as "Motor Voter," which provided for voter registration at state Department of Motor Vehicles (DMV) offices, created a federal registration form, and included provisions meant to sharply curtail voter "caging." However, numerous anecdotal accounts make it clear that caging is still happening despite the NVRA.

The Fourth Mississippi Plan began with Republican officials' backlash to the highly contested election of 2000. Between the Florida recount debacle and outrage over botched election procedures and inaccurate voter rolls in St. Louis, Missouri, Republican Party officials embraced the idea that voter fraud was a widespread problem that required measures such as Proof of Citizenship, Photo ID, and disenfranchisement of those convicted of felonies. Critics never wavered from their contention that little, if any evidence existed to back the claims of voter fraud, but proponents of the new laws were undaunted. Of course, this era has also seen numerous court rulings, with mixed results. Photo ID laws, for example, were upheld in *Crawford v Marion County* (2003), but only under certain circumstances. On the other hand, proof-of-citizenship requirements were sharply limited by the U.S. Supreme Court (*Arizona v Inter Tribal Council* 2013), and in one case, struck down entirely by a Federal District Court (*Fish v Kobach/Bednasek v Kobach* 2018).

The remainder of this book is concerned with empirically testing the impact of the laws and procedures associated with the Fourth Mississippi

Plan, including voter ID, proof of citizenship, felony disenfranchisement, and gerrymandering. Voter "caging" is also discussed in chapter 8. Caging is a process by which postcards or other mailers are sent to specified, targeted precincts, and voters who do not return these by the deadline are removed from the voter rolls. The most egregious forms of caging are supposed to be illegal, as per the NVRA, and it also receives bad publicity when discovered. As a result, it often occurs in the shadows, thus is not as easy to study systematically.

In chapter 3, the author begins by continuing ch. 2's analysis with a more detailed discussion of the laws passed since 2000. The author notes the debate, not only over the laws themselves, but also over how to measure them and whether they are significant. The results of earlier research are mixed. The author then offers his own cross-sectional, county-level data analysis from 2016. The results point to a possible backlash effect among African American voters, finding findings that both non–photo ID and photo ID laws resulted in higher, not lower turnout in the 2016 presidential election. The author also found that the interaction with percentage of African American voters again pointed to higher turnout—the reverse of what was expected, and an indication of a possible backlash effect. The other results—including those that interact the new laws with a county's percentage of Hispanic voters—are insignificant.

In chapter 4, the chapter's author develops the backlash hypothesis further with an analysis of individual-level data. Using American National Election Studies data for the 2012 election, the analysis finds that the presence of a "soft" ID law correlates with a greater likelihood of participants voting, and the impact is even stronger when it is combined with the voter's having been mobilized via personal contact from a campaign. Only one state—Pennsylvania—had such a law taking effect that year, and it was highly controversial. The courts modified the law into a muddle, and one Republican legislative leader even said publicly that the law's purpose was to deliver the state's electoral votes to Mitt Romney. Utilizing two different datasets and two different elections, chapters 3 and 4 offer substantial, if not definitive evidence that a backlash against ID laws may be occurring, particularly among African American voters under certain circumstances.

In chapter 5, the authors analyze the impact of these laws on changes in the partisan vote share and changes in county-level turnout, 2008–12 and 2012–16. As with the two previous chapters, this analysis finds that the imposition of new laws correlates with higher, not lower voter turnout in many cases. Likewise, the impact of the new laws when interacted with percentage Black hints at a possible backlash effect, while the interaction with percentage Hispanic, respectively, are mixed. Yet there is a notable relationship with partisanship—the imposition of the new laws correlates with a larger shift toward Republican votes than in counties located in states that did not have the new laws in place. Thus, while the impact on turnout and racial composition is inconclusive or even (as per the two previous chapters) in the opposite direction than hypothesized, the impact in shifting the electorate toward being slightly more Republican is evident from this analysis. Combined with chapter 3, the overall conclusion appears to be that ID laws may be more effective at mobilizing Republican voters than they are at suppressing Democratic-voting constituencies. However, the evidence also points to a backlash effect among African American voters, who in many cases are more, not less, likely to vote when they live in states affected by the new laws. The impact on Hispanic voters is more mixed.

These puzzling results may be explained in part by research done previously. Smith, Anderson, and Rackaway (2014) found that when certain restrictive laws were put in place, they shifted the electorate, not by suppressing Democratic turnout, but by boosting Republican turnout. In other words, the laws may be an effective voter-mobilization tool for Republicans. The results of chapter 5 are consistent with this finding.

In chapter 6, the author considers the impact of felony disenfranchisement laws, finding that there is a wide variation among the states regarding the impact of these laws. Some states—particularly in the South—effectively ban those convicted of felonies from voting for life, unless they successfully petition the court or governor for a restoration, which must be done on a case-by-case basis. The percentage of the voting-age population (VAP) disenfranchised is highest in these states, reaching its peak in Georgia, where a full three percent of VAP is ineligible to vote due to felony convictions. At the other end of the spectrum are Maine and Vermont, where there is no loss of voting rights even while serving one's sentence, and absentee voting stations are set up inside state prisons. Most states are in between these extremes, denying one the right to vote while in prison or under alternative sentencing, as well as on parole and probation, but then allowing for restoration of these rights upon completion of the sentence. However, popular misunderstanding of the laws by the affected population leads to a widespread belief that they have lost their voting rights for life, even when this is not the case.

Two notable states in the felony-disenfranchisement analysis are Iowa and Florida, which are moving in opposite directions. Iowa recently passed a strict, lifetime felony disenfranchisement law. By contrast, Florida voters approved a 2018 ballot initiative repealing what had been one of the nation's strictest felony-disenfranchisement laws. However, the Florida Legislature has looked at options to limit or override the voter-approved initiative.

The analysis showed that in 2016, a higher percentage of the African American population disenfranchised by these laws correlated with lower voter turnout and a larger shift toward the GOP, relative to 2012. These results were as hypothesized, and they are troubling.

In chapter 7, the authors analyze the mathematical studies on gerrymandering. Mathematical analysis shows that a coherent way of modeling gerrymandering is impossible. One mathematician even showed that an intuitive, geographically compact hypothetical map of North Carolina congressional districts would have even more bias toward the state's slight Republican majority than would the gerrymandered map currently being used. The authors contributed their own model, showing that even a slight partisan majority in a state leads one to predict that most possible ways of drawing districts will result in a heavy bias toward that majority, and then applies this to hypothetical maps of Iowa. Thus, rather than gerrymandering being a tool to "pack" and "crack" minorities, it may make more sense to view gerrymandering as the best hope for minority representation, assuming single-member districts and winner-take-all elections. If anything, gerrymandering tends to benefit the minority. Proportional representation remains the best way to insure minority representation, but it is rarely used in U.S. congressional or state legislative elections.

In chapter 8, the author considers civil rights groups' responses to these new laws, as well as other suppressive tactics used against minorities such as voter caging. The author finds that civil rights groups split into three strategic approaches when fighting these new laws. In the electoral strategy, the civil rights organizations and the Democratic Party utilized voter anger at the laws to mobilize voters, hoping not only to elect more allies but to elect a majority that would vote to repeal the laws. As noted above, chapters 3 and 4 offer prima facie evidence that this strategy may be effective in some cases, particularly with African American voters. In addition, the electoral strategy has also been combined with protest, the second strategy, particularly since the rise of the #BlackLivesMatter movement.

The final strategy was the legal one. Embraced by the NAACP and the ACLU, the legal strategy led to a whole series of court cases challenging the laws. During this time, the results were decidedly mixed. In general, there has been no clear thrust, either pro or con, regarding the constitutionality of these laws, and court rulings often turn on a very detailed reading of each individual law.

Taken together, the studies in the book result in several findings. First, our review of the other studies finds that there is not a strong case for the existence of widespread voter fraud, which is the justification used for passing the laws in the first place. Second, the results regarding the impact on turnout are mixed. None of our analyses found a significant impact on Hispanic voters, and some even pointed to a possible backlash regarding ID laws—an actual boost in turnout—among African American voters, particularly if they are mobilized. Yet we do find that the laws shift the composition of the electorate toward being slightly more Republican. One plausible explanation for this, is that ID laws tend to mobilize Republican voters, rather than demobilize Democrats. However, the analysis of felony disenfranchisement laws indicates that a higher percentage of African Americans disenfranchised correlates lower turnout as well as a larger shift toward the Republican Party.

As for gerrymandering, mathematical analyses offer little hope that drawing more compact districts would increase minority representation—indeed, it may even dilute it. And finally, in the courts, the legal fight is ongoing, with no clear direction being established in favor of, or in opposition to the laws, and the rulings being made on a case-by-case basis, while new civil rights activists have merged together their concerns about restrictive voting laws with a host of other issues such as stopping police brutality, and Medicaid expansion.

A Note on Tone and Consistency

This book is an edited volume. All contributors are academics, including several political scientists, one economist, one mathematician, and one geographer. Every effort has been made to format the chapters consistently and to make references within the chapters to other chapters in this book that are relevant to the discussion. Still, each chapter is written as a standalone piece, even though none of them have been published elsewhere. As a result, some variations in writing style and formatting are to be expected. Still, the editor has made an effort to link the chapters together into a cohesive narrative, so that the book may be read cover to cover and not simply treated as a reference volume.

References

Arizona v. Inter Tribal Council of Arizona, Inc. 570 U.S. 1 (2013).
Bednasek v. Kobach, 259 F. Supp. 3d 1193 (D. Kan. 2017).
Crawford v. Marion County Election Board, 553 U.S. 181 (2008).
Fish v. Kobach, 189 F. Supp. 3d 1107 (D. Kan. 2016).
Smith, M., Rackaway, C., & Anderson, K. (2014). *State Voting Laws in America: Historical Statutes and Contemporary Interpretations*. Palgrave Pivot.

Chapter 2

Black Voting Rights 1865–2016
Two Reconstructions and Four Mississippi Plans

Russell Brooker

During all of American history, there have been disputes about who should be able to vote. Over more than 240 years of independence, people have been enfranchised and disfranchised in an endless game in which no victory or defeat is ever permanent. While the fight over the right to vote has been fought along several axes, including gender, race, and social class, this chapter focuses on voting rights of African Americans since the Civil War.

Voting rights can be given or taken away by at least three mechanisms. The first method is through simply bestowing or restricting the vote legally, either through constitutional provisions, statutory laws, or administrative procedures. The second method is through vote dilution, or affecting the value of people's votes. People are allowed to vote, but their votes are diluted, sometimes to the point that they do not matter. The third method is through illegal actions and usually involves fraud, intimidation, or violence. All of these methods have been used throughout American history, but some have been more important at certain times, while others were more important at other times.

Use of all three methods of expanding or limiting the vote have been controversial and have led to a great deal of litigation. The courts had ruled on practically all the efforts to expand or restrict the franchise through constitutional and statutory provisions, through vote dilution, and through illegal methods.

The original Constitution left voting qualifications up to the states, and before the Civil War, the federal government kept out of suffrage issues and election administration. But soon after the war, with the authority of the Fourteenth and Fifteenth Amendments, the federal government intervened in the voting procedures of the former Confederate states and promoted Black voting. With federal backing, African Americans began voting in large numbers, electing many of their own to local, state, and national offices; this time is called Reconstruction; in this chapter we are calling it the First Reconstruction.

After a few years, in the middle 1870s, there was a violent white reaction that took the vote away from many Black men. This reaction was called the Mississippi Plan. It disfranchised most African Americans, but many continued to vote. After several more years, in the 1890s, a larger, mostly legal movement destroyed almost all Black voting in the South and set up the Jim Crow system of white supremacy. With this second reaction, the name of the 1870s movement was changed to the First Mississippi Plan, and movement 1889–1908 was dubbed the Second Mississippi Plan. African Americans did not sit idly by and accept the loss of their voting rights, but by the early 1900s, Black voting in the South was almost nonexistent.

Over the next 50–60 years, African American activists worked to incrementally increase Black voting, and they were often successful, especially from the 1940s onward. Here, we will refer to his roughly span of time between the Second Mississippi Plan and the Civil Rights Movement of the 1960s as the "Interim." Black voting increased, but in most places in the South that increase was not enough for Blacks to have a significant effect on election outcomes

The Civil Rights Movement of the 1950s and 1960s led to many voting reforms and expansions of the franchise, the most important being the 1965 Voting Rights Act (VRA). In terms of voting, this act ushered in the Second Reconstruction. The federal government sent registrars into the South to register voting-age Black and later monitored Black voting in the following years. The federal Department of Justice (DOJ) was given the power to regulate elections in areas where Black voting had been the lowest and to prevent election law changes likely to disfranchise African Americans. Black voting and officeholding increased dramatically.

Not surprisingly, there was pushback to expansion of Black voting. Beginning with the Mississippi legislature, electoral devices were implemented to render Black votes as insignificant. Whites conceded to African Americans the right to vote, but they worked to make sure that Black votes did not affect the outcomes of elections. With this particular strategy, whites worked to dilute the impact of Black voting, not to deny the right to vote. For the remainder of the twentieth century, African Americans and their allies in the federal government fought a running battle for the right to cast meaningful ballots. Blacks and whites fought over districting, at-large voting, and many other electoral mechanisms for Blacks to vote without their votes counting for much. As far as we know, nobody has ever referred to this conflict as the Third Mississippi Plan, but that is what we call it here.

Beginning in the early 2000s, there was a new era of restrictive voter laws. It appears to have been launched by Republican outrage over two elections in 2000, the presidential election in Florida, with its notorious recounts, and the U.S. Senate election in Missouri, where electoral chaos reigned in the city of St. Louis and the late governor Mel Carnahan was elected to the seat posthumously. Proponents of the new laws argued that they were needed to control voter fraud, while opponents argued that their real targets were African American and Latino voters, particularly those living in large cities in battleground states such as North Carolina, Ohio, and Florida. During this period, these states tended to be competitive in presidential elections while having Republican majorities in their state legislatures, who passed these laws and defended them.

Table 2.1 summarizes the seven time periods included in this chapter.

Table 2.1. Two Reconstructions and Four Mississippi Plans

Main Time Periods	
Name	Years
First Reconstruction	1865–1900
First Mississippi Plan	1875–1877
Second Mississippi Plan	1889–1908
Interim: The Long Fight for the Vote	1909–1964
Second Reconstruction	1965–1982
Third Mississippi Plan	1965–1999
Fourth Mississippi Plan	2000–

The First Reconstruction: 1865–1900

Reconstruction began even as the Civil War was being fought and continued on for more than three decades.[1] During Reconstruction, Black voting began on a massive scale, mainly in the South. For the most part, states outside the South did not allow African Americans to vote. When the Civil War began, six states had Black voting (Maine, Massachusetts, New Hampshire, New York, Rhode Island, and Vermont), and six had had Black voting but had discontinued it (Connecticut, Delaware, Kentucky, Maryland, New Jersey, and Pennsylvania). The other 26 states had never allowed African Americans to vote (Porter, 1918, p. 90).

Immediately after Abraham Lincoln's death, Andrew Johnson took control of Reconstruction. He started a process of quick reunion with the seceding states, with no plans to enfranchise former slaves. However, within a year, Congress, led by Republicans who were much more sympathetic to Black rights, took Reconstruction from Johnson's hands. After Congress took control, Black men were enfranchised throughout the South. In 1868, the Fourteenth Amendment declared that African Americans were citizens of the country and the state where they resided and were entitled to equal protection under the law, and in 1870 the Fifteenth Amendment made it illegal for the national government or any state, North or South, to abridge or deny any citizen the right to vote "on account of race, color, or previous condition of servitude."

The enfranchisement of African American men in the South was a logical product of the Civil War. Republican Senator William Stewart of Nevada, a sponsor of the amendment, said that the Fifteenth Amendment "must be done. It is the only measure that will really abolish slavery. It is the only guarantee against . . . oppression. It is the guarantee . . . that each man shall have a right to protect his own liberty" (Foner, 2006, p. 148). In 1864, before the Civil War ended, African American activists formed the National Equal Rights League (NERL), with Frederick

---

1. By convention, we date the end of Reconstruction in 1877, after an arrangement was made to elect Republican Rutherford B. Hayes and federal troops were withdrawn from the state capitols in South Carolina and Louisiana. However, Reconstruction ended sooner than 1877 in some states, such as Mississippi, and lasted until the end of the century in other states, such as North Carolina. In 1881, Tuskegee Institute was founded in Alabama. The school became possible because a white politician had promised Black voters that he would provide land for a school. George Henry White, an African American, was elected to Congress from North Carolina in 1896 and 1898.

Douglass as its president. The NERL endorsed Abraham Lincoln for president in 1864 and pushed strongly for the right for Blacks to vote. Organized both North and South, it allied with Radical Republicans in Congress and was successful in advocating for the passage of the Fifteenth Amendment (Walton, 1972, pp. 44–47).

Newly enfranchised African American voters elected hundreds of their own number to political posts, including more than 900 state legislators, two U.S. Senators and 14 U.S. Representatives, all of them Republicans (Foner 1993, pp. 268–272). Eric Foner identified 18 state-level elected African American officials, including one governor, five lieutenant governors, two treasurers, four superintendents of education, and seven secretaries of state (Foner, 1988, p. 353). Northern Republicans supported Black enfranchisement efforts because the overwhelming majority of Southern whites at the time were Democrats. Without Black political engagement, there would have been virtually no prospects for a Southern Republican presence.

Reconstruction saw many advances, particularly in public works and education. Between the end of the Civil War and 1900, African Americans and their white allies founded 67 Black universities that still exist today (Brooker, 2017, pp. 16, 43, 109). Black activist W. E. B. Du Bois quoted an African American legislator from South Carolina:

> We were eight years in power. We had built school houses, established charitable institutions, built and maintained the penitentiary system, provided for the education of the deaf and dumb, rebuilt the jails and court houses, rebuilt the bridges, and reestablished the ferries. In short, we had reconstructed the state and placed it upon the road to prosperity. (Du Bois, 1915/2007, pp. 162–163)

The First Mississippi Plan: 1875–1877

Southern white Democrats overwhelmingly opposed Black voting and responded to the Black vote with a variety of tactics, the most important being persistent violence. This reaction has been called the First Mississippi Plan. This plan was not a coordinated scheme; rather, it consisted of individual whites and white organizations working to keep African Americans from voting. It is difficult to definitively say that it began at a specific date in a particular place, but generally it was most prominent in Mississippi and began around the year 1875. The First Mississippi Plan began before Reconstruction ended.

Republican meetings were disrupted, voters were intimidated or killed, and candidates were beaten and assassinated. Ballot boxes were stuffed, and many ballot boxes in Black areas were thrown in nearby rivers. In a few cases, duly elected Black officials were thrown out of office in white coups.[2] White Southern authorities typically tolerated white violence and sometimes participated in it. While Southern Democrats were illegally disfranchising African American men, most white Northern Republicans gave up trying to protect the Black vote and turned their attention to other matters. An anti-Grant faction of the Republican Party, called Liberal Republicans, turned their attention away from Black issues to corruption and the tariff. President Grant, who had supported Black rights, gave up on voting rights in the South and, referring to election battles said he was "tired of these autumnal outbreaks" (Klarman, 2006, p. 37).

Violence was the heart of the First Mississippi Plan, but Black disfranchisement was enhanced by several measures. Probably the most important was the poll tax. While the amount of each tax might be small, poor Blacks and whites simply could not afford any extra expenses and were kept from voting. Literacy tests also kept illiterate Blacks from voting. New, more cumbersome registration laws were passed. If Black voters could not register, they could not vote. One device acted as a de facto literacy test; it involved a separate box for each office, with the order of the boxes shuffled throughout the election day. Illiterate voters could not tell which box was for which office, and white Democratic election officials did not help them. Although different numbers of boxes might be used, this device is often called the "Eight Box" method. Another way that Blacks were disfranchised was through not allowing former lawbreakers to vote. Mississippi reduced the level of theft that resulted in disfranchisement so low that it was said to be the cost of one pig; the law was usually called the "pig law."

The federal courts contributed to the Mississippi Plan and the assault on Black voting. In *U.S. v Crosby* (1871), a federal court ruled on a case in which some white men had entered a registered Black man's home to intimidate him into not voting. The men were arrested on a federal

---

2. The most famous white coup took place in Wilmington, North Carolina, in 1898, but there were other coups in less prominent places.

law, but the court ruled that the constitutional protections did not apply because there was no federal law against breaking into people's homes.

The two most important cases involving voting rights were decided in 1875 and 1876. The first was *Cruickshank v U.S.* (1875). In this case, William Cruickshank and two other white men had been convicted in federal court for participating in a massacre of 60–150 Black Republicans in an election in Colfax, Louisiana. They were arrested on the basis of an 1870 law enacted to enforce the Fourteenth Amendment, which made it illegal to conspire to deprive people of their constitutional rights. The U.S. Supreme Court overturned their conviction because, the justices said, the Fourteenth Amendment was designed to stop states from infringing on people's rights. Since Cruickshank and the two other men were private citizens, not states, the amendment was not relevant; murder cases needed to be tried in state courts. The white government of Louisiana had no intention of prosecuting Cruickshank and his friends, and the Fourteenth Amendment was rendered moot.

The other case was *U.S. v Reese* (1876), in which the Court held that the Fifteenth Amendment did not confer a new right to vote for African Americans, but simply prohibited states from denying the vote on account of race. Two men, Hiram Reese and Matthew Fourchee, had refused to let William Garner, an African American, vote because he had not paid a poll tax, and they would not allow him to pay the tax. The Court ruled that since Reese and Fouchee had discriminated against Garner because he had not paid a poll tax, and the Fifteenth Amendment did not outlaw poll taxes, the Fifteenth Amendment did not apply (Franklin 1961, 208).

However, in one case, the Court did uphold Black voting rights. In *ex parte Yarbrough* (1884) the Court upheld the convictions of eight white men who had tried to intimidate a Black man in Georgia from voting, saying Congress had the constitutional authority to enact an 1870 Enforcement Act. But even with the Yarbrough case to the contrary, clearly *Cruickshank* and *Reese* seriously compromised the constitutional guarantees of voting rights to African Americans in the South.

As Black rights were disappearing, there was one effort to restore them. In 1890 a Northern white Republican, Representative Henry Cabot Lodge of Massachusetts, introduced a Federal Elections Bill to ensure Black voting rights in the South. Called the Lodge "Force" Bill in the South, it was extremely unpopular among white Southerners. Although Republican President Benjamin Harrison supported it, the bill was defeated in Congress in 1892.

The Second Mississippi Plan: 1889–1908

The First Mississippi Plan reduced the Black vote dramatically, but it did not eliminate it. African American men continued to vote in several Southern states and elected Black Republicans to office. The Second Mississippi Plan took votes from virtually every African American man in the South.

Although they had the same goal—disfranchisement of the Black voter—and many of the same methods, the First and Second Mississippi Plans were different. The First Plan was based on violence and backed by law. The Second Plan was based on law and backed by violence. The designers of the Second Plan acknowledged that their efforts had not been complete and a permanent solution was necessary. Historian Michael Perman (2001) quoted a North Carolina newspaper that a disfranchisement amendment would "settle this irritating race question and remove this ever recurring and festering sore on the body politic" (p. 13). He also quoted the chair of the 1900 disfranchising convention in Alabama about the two Plans:

> [T]he great question of the Elective Franchise must be settled. The white line was formed in 1874 and swept the white men of Alabama into power. The white line has been re-formed in 1900 to keep them in power forever. (p. 13)

Writing in 1915, W. E. B. Du Bois made the same point and expanded on it. The goal of the new laws and constitutional changes was to disfranchise African Americans and stigmatize and humiliate them:

> [T]he South strove to make the disfranchisement of the Negroes effective and final. Up to this time disfranchisement was illegal and based on intimidation. The new laws passed between 1890 and 1910 sought on their face to base the right to vote on property and education in such a way as to exclude poor and illiterate Negroes and admit all whites. In fact they could be administered to exclude nearly all Negroes. To this was added a series of laws designed publicly to humiliate and stigmatize Negro blood: as, for example, separate railway cars; separate seats in street cars, and the like; these things were added to the separation in schools and churches, and the denial of redress to seduced colored women, which had long been the custom in the South. All these new enactments meant

not simply separation, but subordination, caste, humiliation, and flagrant injustice. (Du Bois 1915/2007, p. 168)

From 1889 to 1908, all eleven former Confederate states amended or rewrote their constitutions to disfranchise African Americans. Statutory laws and traditional customs supplemented the restrictive constitutions. In addition, the white Southern Democrats used violence to attack the Black vote. Without the violence, these constitutions would not have been adequate to remove the Black vote from politics. By the end of this period, Black voting in the South was rare, with most Black voting taking place in big cities like Atlanta and Memphis. The system spawned by these disfranchisement provisions, and supplemented by a host of discriminatory laws, is called the Jim Crow system.

The first Southern state to incorporate the disfranchisement rules into its constitution was Florida in 1889. The first to write a new constitution was Mississippi in 1890. The last Jim Crow constitution was in Georgia, which added disfranchising amendments in 1908.[3] The new constitutions did not explicitly call for an end to Black voting; such a provision would have been declared unconstitutional by the U.S. Supreme Court as a violation of the Fifteenth Amendment. Instead, the state constitutions made use of provisions that had been used earlier, and they added more. Carol Anderson referred to Mississippi's Plan as "a dizzying array of poll taxes, literacy tests, understanding clauses, newfangled voter registration rules and 'good character' clauses—all intentionally racially discriminatory but dressed up in the genteel garb of bringing 'integrity' to the voting booth" (Anderson, 2018, p. 3). These methods were mainly devised to remove Black voting, but many had the effect of taking poor whites off the voting rolls, which further aided conservative Democratic forces.

J. Morgan Kousser (1974, pp. 45–82) and Paul Lewinson (1932, pp. 80–81) described the most important legal methods. The most important restriction on voting was the poll tax. A prospective voter had to pay a small fee, normally around $1–$2, to vote. In some states, such as Georgia, the poll taxes were cumulative—so that if one had not paid it for the last two or three elections, one would have to pay for all those missed elections to vote. While a tax of $1 or $2 may not seem like much, it was a large imposition for a sharecropper who might have an annual cash income of $100, $50, $10, or zero dollars. Clearly, a sharecropper who was perpetually in debt would not have enough money to pay to vote.

---

3. Oklahoma joined the Union in 1907 and enacted a Jim Crow constitution in 1910.

Poll taxes were made even more onerous by requiring that they be paid six months or nine months before the election. Even voters who could easily pay $2 for the privilege of voting might forget to pay the tax long before the election. Sometimes, Democratic voters were reminded to pay their taxes by the election registrars, while others were not reminded.

Voters in some jurisdictions were required to have property of a certain minimum value, which kept landless sharecroppers, tenant farmers, laborers, and other unpropertied people from voting. Literacy tests were used to keep uneducated potential voters away from the ballot box. Typically, a prospective voter had to read and explain what a section of the state constitution or other document said. The tests could be blatantly discriminatory; a white applicant could be asked to explain a nursery rhyme while an African American could be asked to read the Bible in Latin (Carson, Lapsansky-Werner, & Nash, 2007, p. 316). A white registrar would decide which applicants were "literate." Sometimes "understanding" provisions were included; if a voter understood a section of the state constitution when it was read to him, he could register to vote. Sometimes literacy, or understanding, was used in lieu of property qualifications.

Voting regulations also applied to white voters and would keep them from casting their ballots if strictly enforced. To prevent disfranchising whites, some Southern states wrote exceptions into some laws so that any man, or descendant of a man, who was eligible to vote in 1866—or another year before Black enfranchisement—was eligible to vote, even if other regulations seemed to prevent his voting. This provision was widely known as the "grandfather clause," and became so well-known that it gave rise to the popularly used phrase "grandfathering in." Importantly, there were no grandfather clauses for the poll tax.

A prospective voter might need to show that he was a good citizen by obtaining sworn testimonies or by showing that he had held steady employment for a specified number of years. Sometimes "good character" was used when somebody, typically a white Democrat, did not qualify under property and literacy requirements. States made conviction for certain crimes grounds for not allowing prospective voters to vote. These tended to be crimes that African Americans were considered more likely to be convicted of, including petty larceny and "moral turpitude."

Many of the methods used to disfranchise Blacks involved voter registration. In many jurisdictions, voters were removed from the voting rolls unless they re-registered periodically. Registrars could then make re-registration inconvenient or difficult. Rules could be made complex enough that nobody could register without aid from an official. In at least one state, a prospective voter had to put the required information on a blank piece of paper, with no instructions about which information was required. The voting registrars, virtually all Democrats, were given discretion, and they used it to assist potential voters likely to vote Democratic and hinder or confuse potential voters likely to vote Republican or for another party. In addition, residency requirements were often very long. By not allowing men to register to vote until they had lived in the state or election precinct for months, or even a year, people who moved often were effectively disfranchised.

In addition to laws governing voter eligibility and registration rules, Blacks and poor whites were disfranchised by laws governing the polling places and methods of voting. Multiple boxes were used to confuse illiterate voters, as they had been in the 1870s. The "Australian" ballot began being used widely in the second half of the nineteenth century. Today we call it the secret ballot, and it is used in all elections. Before the Australian ballot was used, parties printed the ballots. A voter would bring his ballot to the poll or get it from a party representative. Anybody watching somebody vote could tell whom he voted for. It might seem odd that a secret ballot could be used for partisan and racist purposes. In fact, the Australian ballot was seen by reformers of the day as a great improvement in elections. But the ballots were, like the multiple boxes, used to penalize illiterate voters. The candidates were often listed in alphabetical order under each office, with no party labels. Voters who could not read found it extremely difficult to vote the way they intended. (If party labels were used, an illiterate Black voter could easily learn to mark his ballot whenever the word "Republican" appeared, but without the labels voting required the ability to read.) Again, election officials might or might not help illiterate voters. Combining multiple boxes and unlabeled secret ballots could make voting a very confusing exercise for illiterate voters. Kousser (1974) wrote, "An ingenious lawmaker could make voting all but impossible" (p. 49).

Southern Democrats had another barrier to Black voting. In addition to discriminatory voting qualifications, abstruse registration rules, and Byzantine voting procedures, there was the white primary. Whereas the laws to stop African Americans from voting in general elections could not explicitly mention race, the rules of the Democratic Party could, and did, have a racial exclusion rule. Only whites were allowed to vote in Democratic Party primary elections. Blacks challenged the white primary as a violation of the Fifteenth Amendment; in response, party leaders said that the party itself was not a state or governmental body. It was, instead, a private organization that could determine its own membership and exclude Blacks, without violating the Fifteenth Amendment. This "private organization" concept was repeatedly attacked, but it was allowed to stand until 1944.

What effect did these new legal and constitutional provisions have on Black voting? Most states did not keep statistics on registration by race, but Louisiana did. In Louisiana in 1896, two years before the disfranchising constitution took effect, 130,344 Blacks were registered to vote. In 1900, two years after it took effect, 5,320 Blacks were registered (Lewinson, 1932, p. 81). All over the South, the number of Black voters plummeted. Blacks were left unable to defend their interests in the political realm, which left them helpless to stop Jim Crow.

All of these laws and constitutional provisions were supplemented by intimidation and violence. African Americans who tried to vote were threatened, beaten, and killed. During the 21 years between 1890 and 1910, approximately 2,000 Blacks were lynched—nobody knows the true number—mostly in the South (US Bureau of the Census, 1960). Although most were not lynched for voting, the threat was always there: any challenge to the system could be fatal. The NAACP's magazine, *The Crisis*, quoted an editorial of the *Arkansas Gazette*, a white newspaper, after a race riot in which hundreds of African Americans were killed, warning Blacks that "their race is in danger of annihilation unless Negroes cease to be led by the lure of Liberty and equal political rights" ("The Real Causes," p. 56).

The white Democrats offered many justifications for disfranchising African Americans, emphasizing Blacks' low educational levels and general unfitness for full citizenship. Racist stereotypes were an integral part of the white argument. One interesting argument was that disfranchisement would be good for the souls of the whites. Before these disfranchisement laws, whites were forced to use illegal means, such as intimidation and violence, that weighed heavily on their consciences. With legal disfranchisement, whites would no longer be forced to act immorally and illegally. In 1889, Colonel B. F. Jones wrote in the *Jackson Clarion-Ledger*,

> The old men of the present generation can't afford to die and leave their children with shot guns in their hands, a lie in their mouths and perjury on their souls, in order to defeat the negroes. The constitution can be made so this will not be necessary. (Wharton, 1947, p. 207)

As it had done earlier in the 1870s and 1880s, the U.S. Supreme Court blessed these constitutions in several rulings. In *Williams v Mississippi* (1898), the Court ruled that the Mississippi constitution did not violate the Fifteenth Amendment's guarantee of voting regardless of race because both whites and Blacks need to pay poll taxes and pass literacy tests. In *Giles v Harris* (1903), the Court ruled on the case of Jackson W. Giles, a literate Black man in Alabama who had been voting for years and was now, after the 1902 Alabama constitution, not allowed to register. The Court said that if the electoral system under the new constitution were fraudulent, as alleged, the Court could not order Alabama to register Giles because then the Court would then be participating in the fraud. In a 1903 Kentucky case, *James v Bowman*, two white men kept a qualified Black man from voting, and the Court ruled that the Fifteenth Amendment applied only to state action, not action by individuals; therefore, the Amendment did not apply in this case, and the United States government did not have jurisdiction.

Interim: Prelude to the Voting Rights Act: 1909–1964

The Second Reconstruction, usually identified with the Civil Rights Movement of the 1950s and 1960s, was many years in the making. African American forces did not surrender or give up the fight. During the imposition of Jim Crow and afterward, Black activists worked consistently to enfranchise African American voters (Key, 1949; Perman, 2001; Riser, 2010; Walton, 1972; 1975, Woodward, 1951). In this section of the chapter, we will look at progress made before the 1965 Voting Rights Act.

In an early victory for the National Association of Colored People (NAACP), the Supreme Court invalidated the grandfather clause (*Guinn v United States* [1915]). Although this was a great symbolic victory for Black voting rights, the grandfather clause was used by only a few states on temporary bases, and its abolition meant very little in real terms.

A substantial victory for Black enfranchisement involved the destruction of the white primary. White Democrats claimed that the Democratic Party, as a private organization, could choose its own members. African American organizations, especially the NAACP-Legal Defense and Education Fund (NAACP-LDF), fought the white primary for years, in a series of court cases. In *Nixon v Herndon* (1927), the Supreme Court ruled that Texas law made the Democratic primary "state action" and therefore subject to the Fifteenth Amendment. Texas changed its laws concerning primaries to give the executive committee of the Democratic Party authority to determine who could vote in the primaries, but this was also struck down in *Nixon v Condon* (1932) because the law that made the Democratic Party independent of the state was, itself, state action. Then the Texas Democratic Party acted on its own initiative as a private organization, and declared that its primaries were open only to white voters. The Supreme Court was satisfied with that arrangement in *Grovey v Townsend* (1935). But in an unrelated Louisiana case, *U.S. v Classic* (1941), the Court ruled that a primary election was an integral part of the electoral process. The NAACP-LDF seized on this ruling and finally won its Texas case in *Smith v Allwright* (1944). From this point, Black voters could not legally be denied the vote in Democratic, or Republican, primaries in any state. Southern states still fought to keep their primary and general elections all white, but with constant Black pressure and some state court decisions that reaffirmed *Smith v Allwright*, Black voting increased over the next two decades. Black organizing and political activities were vital in making sure that *Smith v Allwright* and other Supreme Court decisions were implemented. Organizing was widespread throughout the South, nationally, and statewide by the NAACP and by many local Black voting rights organizations.

In the late 1950s and early 1960s, three civil rights acts addressed Black voting—the Civil Rights Acts of 1957, 1960, and 1964. All three were incremental advances in increasing the Black franchise. The 1957 Act created a Civil Rights Division within the Department of Justice and a Civil Rights Commission with the power to investigate illegal voting suppression and recommend prosecution to the U.S. Attorney General. It also made a provision for the Justice Department to begin civil action for injunctive relief when voting rights were being threatened (May, 2013, pp. 96–97; Stephenson, 2004, pp. 210–211, 318–319).

The 1960 Act instituted procedures for the federal government to intervene on voters' behalf. The process was very cumbersome; a prospective voter had to file a complaint that he or she was being denied the right to vote because of race, and then the government had to obtain a court ruling that that the person was actually being denied the right to vote because of race and that denial was part of a pattern. Then victim of that illegal discrimination could apply for a court order declaring him or her eligible to vote, and the court could hear the application or appoint a panel of registered voters to serve as referees. All of this activity took place with Southern federal judges, many of whom shared the segregationist views of the election officials who were denying the vote to Blacks in the first place (May, 2013, pp. 96–97; Stephenson, 2004, pp. 201–211, 318–319). Not surprisingly, the 1957 and 1960 Acts had little effect on Black voting in the South.

The 1964 Act was principally concerned with other issues, such as public accommodations, employment, and women's rights, but it did affect voting rights by stipulating that a sixth grade education could serve as proof of literacy and outlawing the practice of disqualifying voter registration applications because of minor mistakes (May, 2013, pp. 96–97).

Two Constitutional amendments in the 1960s expanded the franchise. The Twenty-Third Amendment (1961) gave citizens in the District of Columbia the vote in presidential elections. Before 1961, District citizens simply watched presidential elections; after 1961, they voted. The amendment was somewhat compromised by the fact that the District received only three electoral votes even if its population warranted more. In addition, the amendment did not provide any representation in Congress, so the people of D.C. still do not have any senators or representatives, although they do have a nonvoting delegate.

The Twenty-Fourth Amendment abolished poll taxes in federal elections. It removed a barrier to voting that every former Confederate state had used in the twentieth century, although only five still used it in the 1960s (Alabama, Arkansas, Mississippi, Texas, and Virginia). Subsequent statutes and court rulings invalidated the poll tax's evil twin, the literacy test.

Also in the 1960s some Supreme Court decisions enhanced the value of the vote. In these rulings, the Court was not ruling on people's right to vote but on whether their votes would be meaningful—that is, on vote dilution, not vote denial. In 1960, the Court, in *Gomillion v Lightfoot*, invalidated new borders of the city of Tuskegee that the Alabama legislature had drawn. The new borders had changed Tuskegee's shape on the map from a square to a 28-sided polygon. The effect of the new city boundaries was to eliminate many Black citizens but very few white ones. The plan was struck down because it violated the Fourteenth Amendment's guarantee of equal rights and the Fifteen Amendment's prohibition against depriving anybody the vote on the basis of race.

In 1962, the Court ruled in *Baker v Carr* that legislative apportionment was justiciable. Previously the Court had been loath to rule on political questions, but it changed its perspective with this case. In the next year, the Court struck down Georgia's county unit system in *Gray v Sanders*. The county unit system was used in Democratic primary elections and gave each county a certain number of votes, much like the Electoral College gives electoral votes to presidential candidates.

More populous counties had more "votes," but not in proportion to their populations. The most important effect of the system was to give rural voters more influence, fundamentally diluting the votes of city residents, particularly those in Atlanta.

The culmination of vote dilution cases during these years was in two Supreme Court cases in 1964. In *Wesberry v Sanders* the Court said that all Congressional districts in a state must have approximately the name number of people. In *Reynolds v Sims* the Court held that state legislatures needed to make their legislative districts, including state senate districts, approximately equal in population. The Court held that Congressional districts and state legislative districts must reflect "one person, one vote." Before these decisions, many Congressional and state legislative districts were vastly different in populations so that some voters, typically rural ones, had much more power than other voters.

During the early and middle 1960s, African American voter organizing was especially active. One prominent voting campaign was coordinated by the Voter Education Project (VEP), an organization founded with help from the Kennedy administration, with financial support from nonprofit foundations. Working with four major civil rights organizations (the NAACP, the Southern Christian Leadership Conference [SCLC] the Congress of Racial Equality [CORE], and the Student Nonviolent Coordinating Committee [SNCC]) and local Black efforts, the VEP supported many registration drives. The VEP was responsible for almost 800,000 new Black voter registrations by the end of 1964 (King, 1964).

The efforts of Black pressure, from the NAACP, the NAACP-LDF, the VEP, and constant local organizing from the 1910s on bore fruit (Bullock & Lamb, 1984; Lawson, 1976; Smith, 2014; Stanley, 1987). The 1965 Voting Rights Act properly gets credit for increased Black voting, but earlier organizing, Supreme Court rulings, and acts of Congress did make a difference. Black voter registration in the South had been about 3 percent in 1940. It increased to about 12 percent in 1947 and stood at about 40 percent in 1964, on the eve of the Voting Rights Act (Keyssar, 2000, pp. 249, 262). By 1965, the stage had been set for a full assault on Black voting restrictions in the South.

The Second Reconstruction: 1965–1982

The Second Reconstruction[4] is generally considered to include the civil rights movement from the early 1950s until the late 1960s. Here, we will look at the culmination of the movement as far as voting is concerned, the Voting Rights Act (VRA) of 1965.[5] Next to the Civil War amendments, this act was the most important voting measure enacted by the federal government. Although Black voting had increased since the 1920s, especially after *Smith v Allwright* in 1944, by the early 1960s very few African Americans voted in the Deep South. We date the end of the Second Reconstruction as 1982, when Congress revised the VRA to say that "effect," not "intent" was enough to overturn a discriminatory law. We will discuss that law in the next section of this chapter.

The first concern of the VRA was vote denial—who gets to vote and who does not? African Americans were clearly the main target of the VRA, but others benefited as well, including Puerto Ricans, other Latinos, and Native Americans. The Act was also concerned with vote dilution; what should be the value of the vote? The immediate impact of the VRA was in the area of securing the vote for formerly disfranchised people, but most of the VRA's history in the rest of the twentieth century involved vote dilution.

In a celebrated protest in Selma, Alabama, in 1965, Black forces attempting to march to the state capitol in Montgomery were beaten by white police on the Edmund Pettus Bridge. The beating was televised on the same day and stirred up irresistible support for the Voting Rights Act that President Lyndon Johnson had introduced into Congress. The Act, signed by Johnson on August 6, 1965, was very complex and provided for several changes in voting laws in the United States. Among its most important features, the 1965 Voting Rights Act:

- Authorized the Attorney General to send federal election "examiners" who could register people who were qualified to vote but had not been allowed to register because of race (Sections 7, 8, and 9).
- Prohibited states and other jurisdictions from using election practices or procedures that restricted the vote on the basis of race. These practices and procedures included discriminatory

---

4. Some sources that explicitly discuss the Second Reconstruction are Bartley and Graham, 1976; Marable, 2007; Valelly, 2004.

5. There are several excellent histories of the Voting Rights Act, including Brown-Dean Hajnal, Rivers, &White, 2015; Bullock, Gaddie, & Wert, 2016; Grofman and Davidson, 1992; Keech, 1968; Lawson, 1985; Light, 2010, Marable, 2007; McCool (Ed), 2012; Parker, 1990; Rhodes, 2017; Valelly, 2004.

registration procedures, discriminatory redistricting plans, and at-large elections (Section 2). Unlike many of the provisions of the VRA, this section did not have an expiration date.

- Designated certain states and parts of states for special treatment (Section 4). These jurisdictions were subject to closer scrutiny in changing their election laws. Jurisdictions qualified for closer supervision if they met the following criteria:

  o They had used discriminatory election tests or devices on November 1, 1964, and

  o Fewer than 50 percent of voting age adults were registered to vote on November 1, 1964, or fewer than 50 percent of voting age adults had voted in the 1964 presidential election.

  Jurisdictions covered in the original VRA were Alabama, Georgia, Louisiana, Mississippi, South Carolina, Virginia, 39 counties in North Carolina, and specified counties in Arizona and Hawaii.

- Prevented any states covered in Section 4 from enacting any new voting "qualifications or prerequisites to voting, or standard, practice, or procedure with respect to voting different from that in force or effect on November 1, 1964" (Section 5). This part of the Act, called "preclearance," required any covered jurisdiction to get approval from the U.S. Department of Justice or the U.S. District Court for the District of Columbia before making any changes in election laws.

- Prohibited literacy requirements for any prospective voter who had completed sixth grade in a U.S. state or territory, or the District of Columbia, or Puerto Rico (Section 4).[6]

The first goal of the VRA was to make it possible for African Americans to vote in the South. The Act was very successful in opening up registration lists and voting booths to Black voters. Table 2.2

---

6. For a clear summary of the 1965 Voting Rights Act, see Kevin J. Coleman, *The Voting Rights Act of 1965: Background and Overview*, Washington, DC: Congressional Research Service, 2014.

shows the increase in Black registration in the seven states covered in Sections 4 and 5 from March 1965, just before the VRA was passed, to September 1967, two years after it was signed into law. In all seven states taken together, African American registration rose from 29 percent to 52 percent. White registration also rose from 73 percent to 80 percent, a clear rise but not as large as the Black increase.

In addition, the number of African American elected officials increased dramatically after the VRA took effect. Table 2.3 shows the

Table 2.2. Voter Registration in Seven Southern States before and after the Voting Rights Act in Percent

State	Before VRA (March, 1965)		After VRA (September, 1967)	
	White	Black	White	Black
Alabama	69	19	90	52
Georgia	63	27	80	53
Louisiana	81	32	93	59
Mississippi	70	7	92	60
North Carolina*	97	47	83	51
South Carolina	76	37	82	51
Virginia	61	38	63	56
Total	73	29	80	52

*Only 39 of 100 counties were covered in Section 4, but the entire state is shown here.

Note: The seven states are the ones covered by Section 4 of the Voting Rights Act.

Source: U.S. Commission on Civil Rights, *The Voting Rights Act Ten Years After*, Washington, DC: Government Printing Office, 43.

Table 2.3. Number of Black Elected Officials in Seven Southern States after the Voting Rights Act

	Type of Office				
Date	U.S. Congress	State Legislature	County Offices	Municipal Offices	Total
February 1, 1968	0	14	81	61	156
April 1, 1974	1	36	429	497	963

Note: The seven states are the ones covered by Section 4 of the 1965 Voting Rights Act.

Source: U.S. Commission on Civil Rights, *The Voting Rights Act Ten Years After*, Washington, DC: Government Printing Office, 50–51.

number of Black elected officials in the same seven states on February 1, 1968, one election cycle after passage of the VRA, and April 1, 1974, four cycles after.

Soon after the VRA was passed, it was challenged in federal court. In 1966, the validity of Section 4 was challenged in *Katzenbach v Morgan*. The Court upheld Section 4 as a valid exercise of Congress's power to enforce, by appropriate legislation, the provisions of the Fourteenth Amendment. Also in 1966, the Court ruled in *Harper v Virginia Board of Elections* that the equal protection clause of the Fourteenth Amendment precluded the imposition of a poll tax in state elections. Since the Twenty-Fourth Amendment already outlawed poll taxes in federal elections, the effect of this ruling was to outlaw poll taxes in the United States. In 1969, the Court ruled in *Allen v State Board of Elections* that "subtle" laws that diluted citizens' votes were unconstitutional. As we will see in the next section of this chapter, the ruling was vital in the federal government's handling of vote dilution efforts in the Third Mississippi Plan.

The VRA was later reauthorized and amended in 1970, 1975, 1982, 1992, and 2006. The 1975 revision added protection for language minorities for ten years, which was extended for 15 additional years in 1992 (Flores, 2015; McCool, Olson, & Robinson, 2007).

One of the main accomplishments of the VRA, the 1964 Civil Rights Act, and other measures was that they institutionalized the civil rights movement. By the middle 1960s, a significant number of agencies had been established within the federal government. The movement was legitimized in law and governmental units were put there to implement it (Walton, 1988, pp. 1–27).

However, the laws were hardly self-enforcing. Since the establishment of the civil rights bureaucracy, enforcement has been a constant interplay and competition between a variety of stakeholders, including the president, Congress, the Department of Justice, the courts, national and local politicians, voters of different races and ethnicities, and local and national organizations devoted to expanding or contracting the vote. It may seem that because the VRA has been reauthorized five times by large majorities, it has had an easy path. However, those lopsided votes for renewal hid the fact that the law faced determined opposition, who fought vigorously behind the scenes (King-Meadows, 2011).

The Third Mississippi Plan: 1965–2000

For the remainder of the twentieth century, jurisdictions, especially those in the South, tried to evade the intention of the VRA (Kousser, 1999). In the past, most efforts to disfranchise had taken the form of vote denial, but for the last three decades of the twentieth century, most efforts were made toward vote dilution. In vote dilution, voters of all kinds are allowed to vote, but the electoral arrangements are designed to ensure that their votes will not make a difference in an election. The measures intended to dilute the vote were as varied as those intended to deny the vote. Some of the more significant ones were:

Gerrymandering

The word *gerrymandering* goes back to 1812 and usually refers to efforts to help parties or incumbents, but in the United States it has often been used to disadvantage racial minorities (Bositis (ed.), 1998; Canon, 1999; Daley, 2016; Light, 2010; Liptak, 2019; Lublin, 1997; McGann, Smith, Latner, & Keena 2016). District boundaries are drawn so that Blacks or other minorities have less opportunity to elect a proportional number of representatives. Gerrymandering typically takes three forms: with "cracking," minority areas are split between two or more districts so that the minority voters cannot elect their own representatives in any of the districts; with "packing," minority voters are placed in districts so that they are guaranteed the power to elect their own representatives in one or a few districts but have virtually no influence in other districts; and with "stacking," minority areas are paired with larger white areas to create districts with white majorities. Of course, cracking, packing, and stacking may be used at the same time in different parts of a jurisdiction.

At-Large Elections

In a voting jurisdiction, such as a city or a county, instead of having districts, elections are conducted with at-large elections. In an at-large election all the members of a county board or city council would be elected at large by all the voters in the county or city. If the majority of voters were white, all of the elected officials would probably be white. For example, if a city had five districts, three with white majorities and two with Black majorities, the city council would probably include three whites and two Blacks if voting were conducted by district. But if voting were conducted at large, it is most likely that all five council members would be white. Each would win with about 60 percent of the vote.

Multi-Member Districts

These function about the same as at-large elections except that instead of all the representatives being elected by one electorate, groups of representatives are elected in a few districts. It would be easy to make sure that whites constituted majorities in each of the larger districts.

Numbered Post System

In another variant of at-large elections, individual candidates are pitted against other individual candidates. For example, if five seats were up for an at-large election, there would be five one-on-one contests. If the voting population of a jurisdiction were 30 percent Black, the Black voters would not be able to concentrate their vote for one Black candidate. Instead, they would have to vote for five individuals, and it is very likely that white candidates will win all five contests.

Casting the Same Number of Votes as Seats

Another variant of at-large elections required voters in multi-member districts to cast votes equal to the number of offices. For example, if there were nine candidates running for five seats, each voter would be required to vote for five candidates. If only one of the candidates were Black and Black voters wanted to vote only for that that candidate, they would be required to also vote for four white candidates. The effect would also prevent minorities from targeting their votes to specific individual candidates.

Runoff Elections

Many jurisdictions prohibited one-shot election, in which the winner was determined in one voting. Eliminating the one-shot election prevents Black voters from concentrating their votes for one Black candidate. One type of law requires a runoff election if no candidate receives a majority of the vote; if a district is majority-white, white candidates might not get a majority of the votes in the first election, but one white candidate is likely to win a majority in a runoff election were there are only two candidates and one is Black. If a one-shot election were allowed, a Black candidate might get more votes than any of the white candidates.

ANNEXATION

Black voters also had the value of their votes reduced through annexation and de-annexation. Cities, towns, school districts, and other jurisdictions annexed white areas or de-annexed Black areas to ensure victories of white candidates. Black citizens were still able to vote, but not in the districts where they had previously lived.

Just as efforts at vote denial caused a great deal of litigation, efforts at vote dilution also led to much litigation. In 1969, the U.S. Supreme Court ruled in *Allen v Board of Elections* that all changes in the election laws of the affected states, including involving vote dilution, were subject to preclearance in VRA's Section 5. Chief Justice Earl Warren, in the majority opinion, wrote that "Congress intended to reach any state enactment which altered the election law of a covered State in even a minor way" (Davis & Graham, 1995, p. 135). Warren also said that "the Voting Rights Act was aimed at the subtle, as well as the obvious, state regulations which have the effect of denying citizens their right to vote because of their race. . . . The right to vote can be affected by a dilution of voting power as well as by absolute prohibition on casting a ballot" (Parker, Colby, & Morrison, 1994, p. 138).

Subsequent conflicts over vote dilution were played out to a large extent through litigation, with the Supreme Court often deciding the issues. The politics of the Voting Rights Act were influenced by an important case, *City of Mobile v Bolden* (1980). The case involved the governmental structure of Mobile, Alabama, that had been in effect for more than a half-century. Since 1911, the city had used a commission form of government, with three commissioners elected at large. Black citizens in Mobile sued, claiming that the at-large voting system was discriminatory and violated Section 2 of the VRA. Justice Potter Stewart wrote for the plurality of the Court in upholding the commission form of government and the at-large elections. He said that Blacks could register and vote in Mobile "without hindrance" and could run for the office of commissioner and be elected to it. He said proof of discriminatory effect was not enough to indicate that a particular election law was discriminatory. Instead, a plaintiff would have to show that the law was written with the intention to discriminate against voters because of their race. Intent to discriminate is very difficult to prove because lawmakers constructing discriminatory laws rarely announce that their intention is to discriminate. It is easy to think of a nondiscriminatory reason to justify even the most discriminatory laws (Davis & Graham, 1995, pp. 291–293).

Congress reacted to the ruling in its reauthorization and amendment of the VRA in 1982. The new version specified that the Department of Justice did not need to show that a jurisdiction had the intent to discriminate on the basis of race or language; merely showing that a change in an election law would have the effect of discrimination was adequate to be stopped by the DOJ under its preclearance power. This 1982 revision marks the year we have designated as the "end" of the Second Reconstruction. After this year, the Department of Justice had as much authority to enforce the VRA as it was going to get.

In 1986, the U.S. Supreme Court ruled on a case, *Thornburg v Gingles*, in which Ralph Gingles and other African American voters in North Carolina challenged seven state legislative districts, six of which were multimember districts. The provision in the 1982 changes—that only racial effect, not intent, was necessary to find discrimination—led the Court to conclude that the redistricting plan violated Section 2 of the VRA because it illegally diluted the votes of Black citizens (Davis & Graham, 1995, p. 295).

The fight over vote dilution often focused on the creation of majority-minority districts—districts in which minorities constituted the majority of voters. In the South at this time, "minority" usually meant "Black." Some majority-minority districts exist naturally, such as in big city neighborhoods and rural counties, but others have been created by packing as many Black voters into one district that the elected representative is likely to be an African American. The constitutionality of these districts has been continually challenged, with the Supreme Court ruling many times, providing different rulings that parsed the laws ever more finely. Some rulings seemed to support majority-minority districts, and others tended to oppose them. Three cases stand out. In the same *Thornburg v Gingles* (1986) decision, the Court indicated that majority-minority districts are constitutional by identifying three criteria that would justify them: (1) the minority group is sufficiently numerous and compact to constitute a majority in a single district; (2) the minority group is cohesive in that it tends to vote similarly; and (3) the majority bloc can usually defeat the minority group (Keyssar, 2000, p. 294).

However, in two other decisions, the Court was more skeptical. In *Shaw v Reno* (1993) the Court ruled that racial criteria could be used for redistricting but it would need to pass a standard of strict scrutiny, a high standard. In the North Carolina district at hand, the majority opinion said its shape was "bizarre" and looked like "political apartheid." In *Shaw v. Hunt* (1996) the Court said that a North Carolina majority-minority district was unconstitutional because race was the "predominant factor" in drawing the district (Stephenson, 2004, pp. 266–269).

The issue of majority-minority districts has not been resolved. In addition to disputes over whether they are constitutional, there is disagreement over whether they actually help minority voters. People who favor majority-minority districts say that having Black (or, now, Latinx) representatives enhances the power of the voters of that ethnicity. Representatives are more likely to work for the interests of people like themselves.

People who oppose majority-minority districts claim that although Black and Latinx voters might elect their own to office, they will have less influence over representatives who are elected from white districts. The net effect of packing minority voters in a few districts is "bleaching" surrounding districts, whose representatives are unlikely to work for minority interests. The logic is that "bleached" districts are likely to elect Republican representatives, but that Democrats are more likely to work for Black interests. If creating a majority-minority district bleaches three surrounding districts, African Americans are likely to end up with one Democratic representative on their side and three Republicans who will not work for their interests. But if the Blacks were not packed into one district, they might be able to elect two or three Democrats (Thernstrom, 2009). Not surprisingly, Black Democratic representatives in majority-minority districts and Republican representatives in "bleached" districts tend to support majority-minority districts.

Another argument is that because of changes in the American electorate and the effects of the VRA, majority-minority districts are no longer needed. This logic would later be used in 2013 in *Shelby County v Holder* by the Supreme Court when it invalidated the formula in Section 4 of the VRA.

The Fourth Mississippi Plan: 2000–

The VRA was renewed in 2006 for another 25 years—one year ahead of schedule. However, before that renewal, efforts had begun to reduce the size of the electorate, almost entirely by Republicans. Vote dilution was not abandoned, especially in terms of gerrymandering, but the focus expanded to vote denial (Berman, 2015; Browne-Marshall, 2016; Hasen, 2012; King & Smith, 2016; Lichtman, 2018; Overton, 2006; People for the American Way / NAACP 2004; Roth, 2016; Smith, Anderson, & Rackaway, 2014; Waldman, 2016; Wang, 2012). Republicans have claimed that there is widespread fraud in American elections, and the illegal voters need to be purged from the electorate. They have used several measures, discussed below, to stop people from voting, such as making registration more difficult, requiring proof of citizenship or government-issued photo identification cards.

Any discussion of these vote denial initiatives must include the caveat that they have not been especially successful. As the empirical chapters in this book show, the laws have, in some cases, a slight downward effect on voter turnout, but no notable shift in the partisan makeup. Race-specific effects have been ambiguous, and no election has been shown to be decided by the laws. Also, there is substantial evidence for backlash effects to the laws. The Republicans must think the measures are effective, or they would not fight so hard for them. The Democrats must also think they are effective, or they would not fight so hard to stop them. However, that is not what we have found. Even though the new laws bear some resemblance to the laws from the Second Mississippi Plan, they have certainly not had anywhere near a similar effect.

The Democrats have referred to Republicans laws as "voter suppression" laws and have fought against them in state and federal court. The attempts to reduce voting turnout have been aimed almost exclusively at population segments that tend to vote Democratic—those less likely to have driver's licenses or stable home addresses, as well as those more likely to register near to election day. Demographically, the new voting restrictions disproportionately limited the votes of low-income citizens, ethnic minorities such as African Americans and Latinos, senior citizens, and students.

Republicans have not said they intend to constrict the franchise. They have not said they were intentionally disfranchising Democratic voters, although Democrats have clearly been the voters most affected.

Instead, the Republicans have said they want to reduce fraud by people voting two or more times or to prevent ineligible voters from voting. When asked to give examples of fraud in the past that they are trying to prevent in the future, they have seldom been able to identify many, if any, cases.

Democrats have claimed that although there has definitely been election fraud in the past—nobody could seriously deny that—the fraud has not involved duplicate or ineligible voting. Fraud in the past involved elections officials acting illegally—stuffing ballot boxes and adding or subtracting votes after they were cast. Fraud related to actual voting has been more prominent in absentee voting, which the Republican measures do not address.

Efforts to reduce the electorate have involved several devices to limit voter registration by imposing restrictions on who can cast votes at the polling places. Here we identify efforts to limit voter registration and to limit voting at the polling places.

Efforts to limit voter registration include:

Former felons prohibited from voting: Felons have been prohibited from voting in many states for more than a century (Hull, 2006, Manza & Uggen, 2006). Today, two states (Maine and Vermont) allow felons to vote while incarcerated, some states allow them to vote after release, some allow them to vote after they have finished parole and probation, and some keep them from voting for life unless the successfully petition for restoration, which few do. Frequently, laws against felon voting have been politically motivated to stop voters, just as Mississippi's "pig law" was designed to keep Blacks from voting. But even if there were no conscious political motivation, the massive increase in incarceration since the 1980s has had a significant effect on voting, especially voting by Black and Latino men.

Voter purges: Voting jurisdictions routinely purge voting lists of voters who have died or moved. Lately, however, this purging has become more aggressive. Using databases that might or might not be accurate, the names of registered voters have been connected to those of convicted felons. The matches did not have to be perfect for the voter to be stricken from the voting rolls. For example, John A. Jones might have been disfranchised because John B. Jones was a felon. For non-felons, the opposite approach was sometimes taken. For example, John A. Jones might be removed as a voter because he was listed as John Adrian Jones in another spreadsheet.

Restrictions on third-party registrations: Some organizations, such as the League of Women Voters, have long registered voters. In fact, voter registration campaigns have become a regular feature of American elections. However, some states have changed their laws so that third-party voter registration campaigns are so cumbersome, and liable to criminal charges, that the independent organizations have curtailed or abandoned their efforts.

Hurdles to Election Day registration: Some states allow voters to register at the polls. These voters tend to be more marginal voters and tend to have less education and vote Democratic. States that have allowed Election Day registration have cut back.

Efforts to limit voting at the polling places include:

Reducing the time for early voting: In the past few decades, large proportions of people have voted before Election Day. In the 2016 presidential election, about one-third of the voters cast their votes before the day of the election. In response, some states have reduced the number of days in which people can vote. Sometimes Black voters were guided by their clergy directly from Sunday church services to vote, in a move called "Souls to the Polls." In response, some states have since outlawed Sunday voting near Election Day.

Requiring government-issued picture identification cards to vote: Beginning in the early twenty-first century states began to require voters to show government-issued picture identification cards at their polling places, even if they were already registered to vote. Driver's licenses always suffice, so drivers are unaffected by this requirement. In addition, passports and military ID cards are accepted. Student IDs may be accepted, especially if they are from state universities. However, Texas does not accept a student ID from a state university, although it does accept a permit to carry concealed weapons. Critics point out that the motives of the Texas lawmakers are transparent: students tend to vote Democratic, while people who carry concealed firearms tend to vote Republican. States that require government-issued photo IDs allow voters without the required cards to get them, usually at Division of Motor Vehicles (DMV) branches. Of course, it is frequently difficult for people who do not drive to get to DMV branches, especially in rural areas where some counties do not have any DMV branches. Alabama enacted a voter ID law in 2014 and then closed 34 DMV branches in Black-majority counties in 2015 (Marsh, 2015).

Requiring proof of citizenship: Some states began requiring voters to show proof of citizenship, usually in the form of birth certificates, passports, or naturalization papers.

Reducing the number of voting places in Democratic areas: In many areas, often Black and Latinx communities, polling places are closed or consolidated, leaving fewer places to vote. Long lines form and fewer people vote because potential voters give up and go home

Of course, affected parties, especially African Americans, Latinx, and Democrats have gone to court to stop efforts to stop them from voting. Overall, the courts have been mixed on their rulings. Sometimes sympathetic to arguments about voter fraud, and sometimes favorable to arguments against voter suppression laws. One U.S. Supreme Court decision during the first decade of the twenty-first century has helped Republicans in their efforts. In *Crawford v Marion County Election Board* (2008), the Court held that requirements for government-issued picture identification cards were constitutional. These laws accepted regular driver's licenses as voter cards, so only people without licenses were affected. These people tended to be Black, Hispanic, and low-income people who do not own cars. The opponents of the laws said that the requirement for a separate voter card was, effectively, a poll tax. Although the cards themselves were free, the documents needed to get the cards, such as birth certificates, were not.

A second Supreme Court decision was *Shelby County v Holder*, decided in 2013. In this decision, the Court invalidated Section 4(b) of the Voting Rights Act. Section 4(b) contained a formula that determined which jurisdictions were covered by Section 5 and the preclearance provision of the Act. Although Congress had reauthorized the Act for 25 years in 2006—with votes of 390–33 in the House and 98–0 in the Senate—the Court held that the formula had not been revised since 1975 and that circumstances had changed too much since then for it to still be relevant. On the same day as the *Holder* decision, Texas implemented a requirement for a government-issued picture ID that had been held up in the preclearance process. In the post–*Shelby County* environment, state and local authorities can still be sued for VRA violations, but preclearance is no longer available.

In a third ruling, combining *Rucho v Common Cause* and *Lamone v Benisek*, the Court addressed vote dilution in the form of gerrymandering. The decision was handed down in June 2019. *Rucho* was about Republican-biased gerrymandering in Virginia, and *Lamone* dealt with Democratic-biased gerrymandering in Maryland. The Court ruled that partisan gerrymandering was not judiciable—that, as the majority opinion said, "partisan gerrymandering claims present political questions beyond the reach of the federal courts" (Liptak, 2019, p. A1). Whereas the 1962 Court had ruled in *Baker v Carr* that apportionment was subject to judicial review, the 2019 Court ruled that it was not, under these circumstances.

Philosophically, it is not inevitable that specifically Republicans or Democrats would be disadvantaged by gerrymandering, since both parties do it. However, in 2019, the Court's decision was seen as clearly favoring Republicans, because in the early twenty-first century they had been using the practice more effectively. One *New York Times* article two days after the decision was entitled, "Democrats Were Outraged, the Republicans Were Thrilled, but It's Far From Over" (Astor, 2019).

Indeed, it is not over. This June 2019 ruling was merely the latest incident in the struggle over vote denial and vote dilution. It was definitely not the last.

Conclusion

In most of American history, the power to vote has been in dispute—whether people would be allowed to vote. But in the time between passage of the Voting Rights Act and the twenty-first century, voting issues tended to focus on the value of the vote, not the right to vote itself. Now, we are back to disputing the power to vote.

In the early twenty-first century, social and electoral trends point to more aggressive attempts to manipulate the franchise. Although one is hard-pressed to find a time in history when politics was kind and gentle, the political environment seems more partisan and polarized than in past generations. The ideological, cultural, and, racial divisions reinforce each other and are reshaping the electoral landscape (Abramowitz, 2018, pp. 1–18). Of these three divisions, the racial one seems the most pronounced. Khalilah Brown-Dean et al. point out that over the past few decades African Americans, Latinx, and Asian Americans have shifted to the Democratic Party while whites have moved "inexorably" to the Republican Party, both in voting and party identification. They also note that in many local elections, "Race seems to divide voters more than other characteristics," including party identification (Brown-Dean, Hajnal, Rivers, & White, 2015, pp. 17–20). Increasing polarization, coupled with recent Supreme Court decisions, appears likely to exacerbate the fight over the franchise.

This short history has shown the never-ending struggle between forces who would expand the vote and those who constrict it. This history has covered African American voting rights, but there are other struggles for the vote, including women, Latinx, and Native Americans. The issue of suffrage is complex, contentious, and ongoing. The following chapters of this book detail empirical findings regarding many of the new laws passed during this, most recent era.

References

Abramowitz, A. I. (2018). *The great alignment: Race, party transformation, and the rise of Donald Trump*. Yale University Press.

Anderson, C. (2018). *One person, no vote: How voter suppression is destroying our democracy*. Bloomsbury.

Astor, M. (2019). "Democrats were outraged, the Republicans were thrilled, but it's far from over." *The New York Times*, June 29, A11.

Bartley, N. V., & Graham, H. D. (1976). *Southern politics and the second reconstruction*. Johns Hopkins University Press.

Berman, A. (2015). *Give us the ballot: The modern struggle for voting rights in America*. Picador.

Bositis, D. A. (Ed.) (1998). *Redistricting and minority representation*. Joint Center for Political and Economic Studies.

Brooker, R. (2017). *The American civil rights movement 1865–1950: Black agency and people of good will*. Lexington Books.

Brown-Dean, K., Hajnal, Z., Rivers, C., & White, I. (2015). *50 years of the voting rights act: The state of race in politics*. Joint Center for Political and Economic Studies.

Browne-Marshall, G. J. (2016). *The voting rights war: The NAACP and the ongoing struggle for justice*. Rowman & Littlefield.

Bullock, C. S., III, & Lamb, C. M. (Eds.) (1984). *Implementation of civil rights policy*. Brooks/Cole.

Bullock, C. S., III, Gaddie, R. K., & Wert, J. J. (2016). *The rise and fall of the voting rights act*. University of Oklahoma Press.

Canon, D. T. (1999). *Race, redistricting, and representation: The unintended consequences of black majority districts*. University of Chicago Press.

Carson, C., Lapsansky-Werner, E. J., & Nash, G. B. (2007). *The struggle for freedom: A history of African Americans, Vol. II*. Pearson Education.

Coleman, K. J. (2014). *The voting rights act of 1965: Background and overview*. Congressional Research Services.

Daley, D. (2016). *Ratf**ked: The true story behind the secret plan to steal America's democracy*. Liveright.

Davis, A. L., & Graham, B. L. (1995). *The Supreme Court, race, and civil rights*. Sage.

Du Bois, W. E. B. (1915/2007). *The Negro*. Forgotten Books.

Editors. (1919). "The real causes of two race riots." *The Crisis*, IXX, 56.

Flores, H. (2015). *Latinos and the voting rights act*. Lexington Books.

Foner, E. (1988). *Reconstruction: America's unfinished revolution: 1863–1877*. History Book Club.

Foner, E. (1993). *Freedom's lawmakers: A directory of black officeholders during reconstruction*. Oxford University Press.

Foner, E. (2006). *Forever free: The story of emancipation and reconstruction*. Alfred A. Knopf.

Grofman, B., & Davidson, C. (Eds.) (1992). *Controversies in minority voting: The voting rights act in perspective*. Brookings.

Hasen, R. L. (2012). *The voting wars: From Florida 2000 to the next election meltdown*. Yale University Press.

Hull, E. A. (2006) *The disfranchisement of ex-felons*. Temple University Press.
Keech, W. R. (1968). *The impact of Negro voting: The role of the vote in the quest for equality*. Rand McNally.
Key, V. O., Jr. (1949). *Southern politics in state and nation*. Vintage Books.
Keyssar, A. (2000). *The right to vote: The contested history of democracy in the United States*. Basic Books.
King, D. S., & Smith, R. M. (2016). The last stand? Shelby County v. Holder, white political power, and America's racial policy alliances. *Du Bois Review, 13*(1), 25–44.
King, M. L., Jr. (1964). *Why we can't wait*. Signet Classics. Retrieved from https://kinginstitute.stanford.edu/encyclopedia/voter-education-project-vep.
King-Meadows, T. D. (2011). *When the letter betrays the spirit: Voting rights enforcement and African American participation from Lyndon Johnson to Barack Obama*. Lexington Books.
Klarman, M. J. (2006). "The Supreme Court and disfranchisement." R. M. Valelly (Ed.), *The voting rights act: Securing the ballot* (pp. 37–56). CQ Press.
Kousser, J. M. (1974). *The shaping of southern politics: Suffrage restriction and the establishment of the one-party south, 1880–1910*. Yale University Press.
Kousser, J. M. (1999). *Colorblind injustice: Minority voting rights and the undoing of the second reconstruction*. University of North Carolina Press.
Kropf, M., & Kimball, D. C. (2012). *Helping America vote: The limits of election reform*. Routledge.
Lawson, S. F. (1976). *Black ballots: Voting rights in the south, 1944–1969*. Columbia University Press.
Lawson, S. F. (1985). *In pursuit of power: Southern blacks and the electoral politics, 1965–1982*. Columbia University Press.
Lewinson, P. (1932/1959). *Race, class, and party: A history of Negro suffrage and white politics in the south*. Grosset & Dunlap.
Lichtman, A. J. (2018). *The embattled vote in America: From the founding to the present*. Harvard University Press.
Light, S. A. (2010). *The law is good: The voting rights act, redistricting, and black regime politics*. Carolina Academic Press.
Liptak, A. (2019). "Court, ruling 5–4, gives green light to gerrymandering: Finds it has no role." *The New York Times*, June 28, pp. A1, A13.
Lublin, D. (1997). *The paradox of representation: Racial gerrymandering and minority interests in Congress*. Princeton University Press.
Manza, J., & Uggen, C. (2006). *Locked out: Felon disfranchisement and American democracy*. Oxford University Press.
Marable, M. (2007). *Race, reform, and rebellion: The second reconstruction and beyond in black America, 1945–2006* (3rd ed.). University Press of Mississippi.
Marsh, R. (2015). "DOT launches investigation in Alabama over DMV closings." *CNN Politics*. December 9.

May, G. (2013). *Bending toward justice: The voting rights act and the transformation of American democracy*. Basic Books.

McCool, D. (Ed.) (2012). *The most fundamental right: Contrasting perspectives on the voting rights act*. Indiana University Press.

McCool, D., Olson, S. M., & Robinson, J. L. (2007). *Native vote: American Indians, the voting rights act, and the right to vote*. Cambridge University Press.

McGann, A. J., Smith, C. A., Latner, M., & Keena, A. (2016). *Gerrymandering in America: The House of Representatives, the Supreme Court, and the future of popular sovereignty*. Cambridge University Press.

Overton, S. (2006). *Stealing democracy: The new politics of voter suppression*. Norton.

Parker, F. R. (1990). *Black votes count: Political empowerment in Mississippi after 1965*. University of North Carolina Press.

Parker, F. R., Colby, D. C., & Morrison, M. K. C. (1994). "Mississippi." C. Davidson & B. Grofman (Eds.), *Quiet revolution in the south: The impact of the voting rights act, 1965–1990* (pp. 136–154). Princeton University Press.

People for the American Way / National Association for the Advancement of Colored People. (2004). *The long shadow of Jim Crow: Voter intimidation and suppression in America today*. Author.

Perman, M. (2001). *Struggle for mastery: Disfranchisement in the south 1888–1908*. University of North Carolina Press.

Porter, K. H. (1918). *A history of suffrage in the United States*. University of Chicago Press.

Riser, R. V. (2010). *Defying disfranchisement: Black voting rights activism in the Jim Crow south, 1890–1908*. Louisiana State University Press.

Rhodes, J. H. (2017). *Ballot blocked: The political erosion of the voting rights act*. Stanford University Press.

Roth, Z. (2016). *The great suppression: Voting rights, corporate cash, and the conservative assault on democracy*. Crown.

Smith, J. D. (2014). *On democracy's doorstep: The inside story of how the Supreme Court brought "one person, one vote" to the United States*. Hill & Wang.

Smith, M. A., Anderson, K., & Rackaway, C. (2014). *State voting laws in America: Historical statutes and their modern implications*. Palgrave Pivot

Stanley, H. W. (1987). *Voter mobilization and the politics of race: The south and universal suffrage, 1952–1984*. Praeger.

Stephenson, D. G. Jr. (2004). *The right to vote: Rights and liberties under the law*. ABC-CLIO.

Thernstrom, A. (2009). *Voting rights—and wrongs: The elusive quest for racially fair elections*. AEI Press.

U. S. Bureau of the Census. (1960). *Historical statistics of the United States, colonial times to 1957*. Author.

Valelly, R. M. (2004). *The two reconstructions: The struggle for black enfranchisement*. University of Chicago Press.

Waldman, M. (2016). *The fight to vote*. Simon & Schuster.

Walton, H., Jr. (1972). *Black political parties: An historical and political analysis.* The Free Press.
Walton, H., Jr. (1975). *Black republicans: The politics of the black and tans.* The Scarecrow Press.
Walton, H., Jr. (1988). *When the marching stopped: The politics of civil rights regulatory agencies.* State University of New York Press.
Wang, T. A. (2012). *The politics of voter suppression: Defending and expanding Americans' right to vote.* Cornell University Press.
Wharton, V. L. (1947). *The Negro in Mississippi 1865–1890.* Praeger.
Woodward, C. V. (1951). *Origins of the new south 1877–1913.* Louisiana University Press.

Court Cases

Allen v. State Board of Elections 393 US 344 (1969)
Baker v. Carr 369 US 186 (1962)
Benisek v. Lamone 585 US _____ (2018)
City of Mobile v. Bolden 446 US 55 (1980)
Crawford v. Marion County Election Board 553 US 181 (2008)
Ex parte Yarbrough 110 US 651 (1884)
Giles v. Harris 189 US 475 (1903)
Gomillion v. Lightfoot 344 US 339 (1960)
Gray v. Sanders 372 US 368 (1963)
Grovey v. Townsend 295 US 45 (1935)
Guinn v. United States 238 US 347 (1915)
Harper v. Virginia Board of Elections 383 US 663 (1966)
James v. Bowman 190 US 127 (1903)
Katzenbach v. Morgan 384 US 641 (1966)
Lamone v. Benisek 588 US _____ (2019)
Nixon v. Condon 286 US 73 (1932)
Nixon v. Herndon 273 US 536 (1927)
Reynolds v. Sims 377 US 533 (1964)
Rucho v. Common Cause 585 US _____ (2019)
Shaw v. Hunt 517 US 899 (1996)
Shaw v. Reno 509 US 630 (1993)
Shelby County v. Holder 570 US 529 (2013)
Smith v. Allwright 321 US 649 (1944)
Thornburg v. Gingles 478 US 30 (1986)US v. Classic 313 US 299 (1941)
Westberry v. Sanders 376 US 1 (1964)
Williams v. Mississippi 170 US 213 (1898)

Chapter 3

The Impact of Voter ID Laws on County Turnout in the 2016 Presidential Election

Ryan E. Voris

The Controversy of Requiring Photo ID

Elections are the most direct link between citizens and their government, and even the most minimal definitions of democracy require elections to be both free and open to all segments of society. In the United States, citizens are confronted with elections that enable them to have a say in who their elected officials are, from the local school board to the president, and in policy decisions through state constitutional amendments, initiatives, referendums, and tax levies. It is not surprising that most battles for civil rights centered on access to the ballot box to allow groups to directly pressure the government for their concerns. The broad swath of election reform in the United States has thus been characterized by expanding access to voting rights; from the fall of property requirements in the early 1800s, to the Civil Rights Movement of the 1960s, and the expansion of absentee and early voting in the 1990s.

Numerous reforms have dramatically increased the ease with which citizens can both register to vote and cast their ballot in elections. However, some argue these reforms open the door to election fraud and other irregularities. While many dispute this claim, issues with the 2000 presidential election recount in Florida provided the motivation for broad steps to both modernize elections in America and protect voter confidence in the electoral system. One reform, championed by Republican officials, was the requirement of photo identification of all voters. In 2002, the U.S. Congress passed the Help America Vote Act (HAVA) to provide federal assistance to states in the hopes of spurring further reform by the states. One provision required all first-time voters to present some form of identification at the polls. Shortly after this, multiple states began to require ID of all voters. In 2006, Indiana became the first state to require government-issued photo ID of all voters. Supporters of the requirement argued that the ID requirement was necessary to prevent election fraud from impacting the election outcome, while opponents raised concerns about the large number of minorities who lacked access to photo ID.

National surveys often show that many citizens express concerns about the potential for voter fraud. Following a survey of voters in the 2008 U.S. presidential election, Alvarez et al. (2009) found that 8.1 percent of voters believed that voter fraud was "very common" in American elections, with a further 17.4 percent believing fraud happened occasionally (10). Additionally, roughly one in five voters were unsure how common voter fraud was and that vote theft and voter impersonation were common in elections (Alvarez et al., 2009, pp. 10–11). Pastor et al. (2010) estimated that 16.6 percent of individuals either saw or heard of fraud at their own polling place and nearly 64 percent reported hearing about fraud at another polling place (475). Despite these reports, much research shows that actual occurrences of voter fraud are rare and do not pose a threat to election outcomes (Minnite, 2010).

If there is seemingly no cause to require ID, critics maintain that ID requirements are intended to reduce turnout among specific segments of the population. The initial HAVA ID requirement faced such strong opposition from Senate Democrats that it was softened from the initial proposal of a photo ID requirement for all voters to a wide range of IDs for first-time voters. Yet, after HAVA seemingly gave approval to ID requirements in general, multiple Republican-controlled states moved to require ID of all voters. In many instances these requirements passed without a single Democratic vote (Hicks et al., 2015; Biggers & Hanmer, 2011). Chief among the critics' concerns is that millions of citizens, particularly minorities, lack access to government-issued photo ID. The American Civil Liberties Union estimates that more than 21 million citizens, and as many as one in four African Americans, would be denied a ballot under many photo ID requirements. Many researchers have likewise found that racial minorities, the elderly, college-age, and low-income voters are less likely to have photo IDs than other segments of society (Pastor et al., 2010; Hershey, 2009; Baretto, Nuno, & Sanchez, 2008).

ID laws have become increasingly controversial as more states have enacted them for all voters and issues regarding access to ID remain a concern. As of early 2020, 34 states ask voters to present some form of identification at the polls on Election Day. Election years are always a time for change in election laws. In 2016, North Carolina and New Hampshire were both set to enact photo ID requirements for the first time, joining 17 other states with similar requirements. Looking forward to the 2020 Presidential Election, several states have made changes to their ID requirements since the last presidential election. Surprisingly, the impact of these laws on political participation remains unclear. Heavy suspicion is that they are enacted by partisans seeking to strategically manipulate the electorate, but do they prevent citizens from participating in elections? Given the widespread concerns about access to ID, do they encourage a backlash effect that mobilizes those otherwise expected to be negatively impacted? Looking at turnout in the 2016 election we can see how these laws impact participation and place ID laws into the strategic context of how political parties use election laws to increase their chances of winning.

Growth of Voter Photo ID Requirements in the United States

By and large, elections in the United States are controlled by the individual states, with enforcement controlled by county governments. The U.S. Constitution provides some guidance on which classes of individuals cannot be *denied* a ballot but gives no specifics on how elections are run. Particularly after the end of Reconstruction, Southern states began revising their constitutions to actively prevent African Americans from voting. While these methods are detailed in other places in this volume, requiring voters to prove their identity at the polls has only recently become a focus of national attention.

Prior to the 2000 presidential election only 14 states had any laws regarding proof of identity at the polls on Election Day. Most of these laws simply asked voters to present some documentation with both their name and address. Only four states, Florida, Hawaii, Louisiana, and Michigan, specified that the ID contain a picture of the voter. Each of these laws also provided some opportunity for individuals without proper ID to cast a ballot without further action by the voter (Bigger & Hanmer, 2011). In most other states voters gave their name to the poll worker and/or signed into the poll book on arriving. Several states checked to ensure the signature from the poll book matched the signature on record, but most simply required poll workers to confirm the name given was on the registration list.

Historically, this was enough to prevent large-scale abuses of the election process. Voting in early America was difficult, and participation was often limited to a small number of urban elites (McDonald, 2010). Low mobility also made it easier for the political parties to police eligibility requirements and ensure only eligible voters were given a ballot (Keyssar, 2000). As the electorate expanded, greater efforts to police eligibility were needed. A key progressive reform during the early 1900s was to require voters to register prior to the election, an effort seen as necessary due to the rampant voter fraud associated with many big city political machines. McDonald (2010) even notes that voter fraud is seen as an explanation for high rates of participation at the turn of the century.

These concerns were renewed in the minds of many following the controversial 2000 presidential election in Florida. Election night saw multiple media outlets award the presidency to then vice president Al Gore (D), only to rescind it moments later and award it to Texas governor George W. Bush (R), and then withdraw again and declare the race too close to call. The final tally was decided by a mere 930 votes and triggered an automatic recount under Florida law. National attention quickly centered on several counties with widespread complaints about how the election was managed (Blaz, 2000).

For several weeks, media coverage centered on the manual recount underway as the courts weighted competing claims on the legality of the recount. The Gore campaign sought to prevent the state from certifying Bush as the winner before the recount was finished while the Bush campaign argued to halt the recount over the lack of statewide standards in how ballots should be counted. After nearly a month the recount was halted by a 5–4 U.S. Supreme Court decision that resulted in Bush being certified as the winner of Florida's electoral votes and thus the presidency. Writing in dissent, Justice John Paul Stevens voiced concerns that the decision would "cast a cloud on the legitimacy of the [2000] election" and future elections (*Bush v Gore* [2000], Stevens dissenting, p. 2).

After the election, the new Congress took the lead in searching for ways to modernize and improve the electoral system. The resulting Help America Vote Act of 2002 (HAVA) included multiple reforms and aid to states designed to improve the reliability and integrity of the election process. One of these reforms was an ID requirement for all voters. While the initial bill passed the U.S. House of Representatives easily, in a 362–63 vote, the initial photo ID requirement for all voters quickly become controversial. Opposition to the photo ID requirement was led by New York Senators Hillary Clinton (D) and Chuck Schumer (D) over concerns that any ID requirement would primarily serve to disenfranchise otherwise eligible voters. Senator Clinton noted that this would have a particularly strong effect among the millions of newly naturalized citizens living in New York and the millions of citizens nationwide who lacked a driver's license (Pear, 2002). HAVA's ID requirement was softened to allow multiple forms of ID and to apply only to first-time voters in federal elections. The revised version passed easily in both houses of Congress, a 357–48 vote in the House and 92–2 in the Senate. It was signed into law by President Bush in October 2002.

After the passage of HAVA, several states adopted similar requirements for all voters. Most of these laws asked voters to present any form of ID that contained both their name and address, and each law contained provisions that enabled those without acceptable ID to cast a regular ballot in the election. Just a few years later, in 2006, nearly half of all states asked voters for some form of ID at the polls (NCSL, 2016). The number of states asking specifically for photo ID remained relatively constant, with only South Dakota passing a photo ID law in 2003. Like the photo ID laws in other states, South Dakota allows voters without photo ID to sign an affidavit of identity and still cast a regular ballot (S.D. Codified Laws §12-18-6.1, 6.2).

The 2004 election was the first national election in which many of the provisions of HAVA had been put into place by states. The Commission on Federal Election Reform, headed by former Republican secretary of state James Baker and former Democratic president Jimmy Carter, was established to review the progress of HAVA reforms and recommend further reforms, if needed. Attention again turned to the necessity of photo ID requirements, as the commission recommended all states move to require photo ID. While the commission was careful to point out that voter fraud was not a major problem facing U.S. elections, they did see photo ID requirements as inspiring broader confidence in the electoral system (Commission, 2005, p. 18). The commission also held than any photo ID law should be accompanied by additional reforms to guarantee all eligible voters are able to gain access to acceptable ID. Buoyed by this recommendation, two states promptly enacted laws requiring government-issued photo ID of all voters in state elections: Georgia and Indiana.

Indiana's law quickly became the focal point for the debate surrounding voter photo ID requirements. Unlike previous laws, Indiana *required* photo ID for all voters and made no provisions for those without acceptable ID to cast a regular ballot. Voters without photo ID would be required to cast a provisional ballot that would only be counted if the individual returned to the local board of elections within 10 days of the election with acceptable ID. Additionally, unlike HAVA or previous ID laws, Indiana's law passed without a single Democratic vote amid overwhelming criticism that the law was primarily intended to disenfranchise key segments of the Democratic constituency. Civil rights groups estimated that as many as 13 percent of Indiana voters lacked acceptable photo ID and that these voters were predominantly African American (Urbina, 2008).

Unable to stop the law's implementation in the 2006 elections, groups quickly moved to challenge the law as an unconstitutional barrier to voter participation. The principal case, *Crawford v Marion County Board of Elections*, reached the U.S. Supreme Court in the summer of 2008 after lower federal courts found little evidence that the Indiana photo ID law prevented anyone from voting in the 2006 election. The case took on added significance as several states were actively considering photo ID requirements modeled on the Indiana law.

Critics argued the effects of the law would serve predominantly to disenfranchise minority, low-income, and elderly voters who lacked access to government-issued photo ID. While the law did make free voter ID cards available to those in need, these cards often required multiple documents and a trip to the Bureau of Motor Vehicles office to obtain the card. In Indiana, this could require up to five different documents to establish the individual's identity, legal status in the United States, Social Security Number, and Indiana residency (IN Sec. of State, 2014). While some documents may fit multiple categories, such as being able to prove both identity and legal status, all documents were required to be either originals or certified copies. Some of these supporting documents might require payment, such as the cost of obtaining a certified copy of one's birth certificate, creating indirect financial costs to the free voter ID card. Additionally, there were opportunity costs associated with visiting the BMV during regular business hours to obtain the ID cards. Critics noted these barriers would be especially burdensome to racial minorities and effectively created a twenty-first-century poll tax that would primarily disenfranchise many minority voters.

Indiana argued that photo ID was necessary to prevent voter fraud and to help maintain voter confidence in the broader electoral system. While there is little evidence that voter fraud plays any role in most elections (Hood & Gillespie, 2012; Minnite, 2010), this remains an area of concern for many voters (Pastor et al., 2010). Indiana pointed to historical incidents of voter fraud, particularly in the northwestern part of the state, to justify the need for an ID requirement. It was also pointed out that there was no evidence that any Indiana voters were permanently denied a ballot in the election. While several voters experienced problems with ID at the polls, most were eventually given a regular ballot which was cast in the election. Two citizens were permanently denied a ballot, but this was due to problems with their registration rather than the lack of photo ID. Supporters argued there was no evidence of any disproportionate impact and the law was a legitimate attempt to improve election management.

In a 6–3 decision, the U.S. Supreme Court largely sided with the state of Indiana, upholding the constitutionality of photo ID requirements. Writing for the majority, Justice John Paul Stevens noted that any restrictions on the right to vote must be both neutral in their application and directly related to voting (citing *Harper v Virginia* [1966]). Additionally, restrictions must not show any evidence of disproportionate impacts to be upheld. Relying on lower court fact finding, the Supreme Court noted that there was little evidence of anyone being denied a ballot and that efforts to maintain voter confidence had an "independent significance" even in the lack of direct evidence of voter fraud (*Crawford v Marion County* [2008], p. 13).

The Court used several recent actions by the federal government to provide additional justification for the photo ID requirement. HAVA showed that federal government saw identification requirements as a means to safeguard the election process. While the act only required ID of first-time voters and allowed for a wide range of possible identification documents, neither did it *prevent* the states from going farther and requiring photo ID of all voters. Additionally, HAVA specifically mentioned photo ID, which the Court took as evidence that a photo ID requirement provided an "effective method of establishing a voter's qualification to vote" (*Crawford v Marion County* [2008], p. 9). Further, the Commission on Federal Election Reform had made specific recommendations about the adoption of photo ID requirements, in conjunction with other reforms, to improve voter confidence. While the report also stated that fraud was not a significant problem in most elections, it also noted that voter fraud might play a major role in close elections if not prevented.

Importantly, the Court did not reject the claims of those challenging the law. The majority in *Crawford* specifically noted that requiring a photo ID does complicate the voting process and create additional barriers to voter participation. However, the Court held these barriers did not appear to be significant for most voters and there was limited evidence of any disproportionate impact. Justice Stevens even commented specifically that given widespread access to driver's licenses in modern society a photo ID requirement presented no greater inconvenience than for many other daily activities. This minor difficulty could then be justified by the state's interest of "carefully identifying all voters participating in the election process" (*Crawford v Marion County* [2008], p. 12).

This left open the possibility of further legal challenges to photo ID requirements on the grounds of access to acceptable ID. Judge Richard Posner, author of the appellate decision largely upheld by *Crawford*, has since raised concerns with photo ID requirements given the uncertainty surrounding access to photo ID and the limited, often conflicting, evidence of how these laws impact voter participation (Posner, 2013). Several state courts have specifically focused on the lack of significant state effort to ensure the universal availability of appropriate ID to strike down photo ID laws in several states. Pennsylvania, for example, made national headlines leading up to the 2012 presidential election when the Commonwealth Court of Pennsylvania struck down a photo ID law modeled after Indiana's. In the decision, the judges specifically focused on Pennsylvania's failure to both educate voters about the new ID requirements and take effort to ensure all voters had acceptable photo ID before the election (*Applewhite v Pennsylvania* [2014]).

At this point it is important to note that since the *Crawford* decision the adoption of ID laws, both photo ID and non–photo ID requirements, has been concentrated nearly entirely in states under

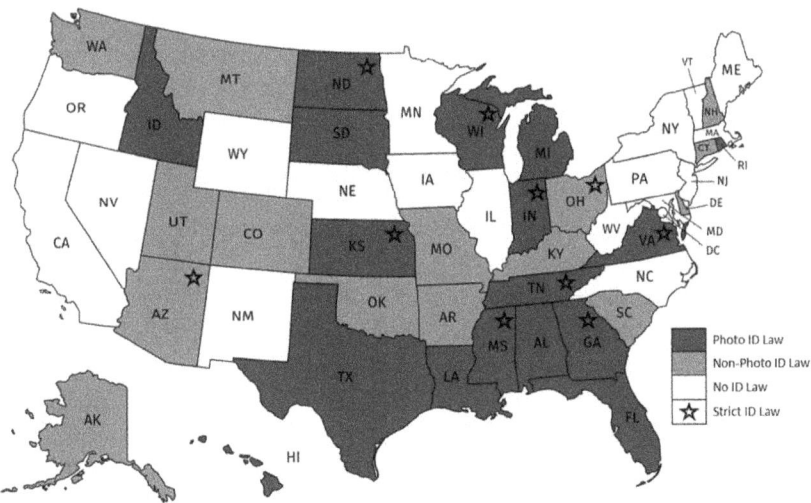

Figure 3.1. ID Laws in U.S. States, 2016.

unified Republican control. Since 2008, Rhode Island is the only state not controlled by Republican officials to enact an ID law. The 2010 elections gave Republicans control of state legislatures in 26 states, placing a total of 20 states under unified Republican control. Since 2010 there has also been the greatest growth in ID requirements, with the number of photo ID laws more than doubling from seven in 2008 to 17 in 2016. Three additional states had passed photo ID laws only to have them struck down by either state courts (Arkansas and Pennsylvania) or federal courts (North Carolina). It is not surprising that the passage of ID laws correlates highly with the number of Republicans in the state house. Hicks et al. (2014) further found that the electoral margin was a key driver of passage, with Republicans in electorally competitive states more likely to pass ID laws than Republicans in uncompetitive states.

Searching for an Impact: Photo ID Laws and Voter Turnout

During the 2016 election more than half of all states asked voters for some form of identification at the polls prior to handing them a ballot. Figure 3.1 details the breakdown of laws in effect during the election: 32 states had laws in effect with 17 of these laws specifically requiring photo ID (NCSL 2016). New Hampshire, North Dakota, and Virginia had ID laws in effect for the first time. It should also be noted that this figure does not include states that had passed an ID law but that did not have that law in effect during the election (West Virginia passed a photo ID law in 2016 to be implemented in 2018; North Carolina and Texas each had photo ID laws struck down in July 2016).

The National Conference of State Legislatures (NCSL) divides ID laws along several dimensions, and this division is most used when discussing voter ID laws. The first dimension is whether the ID laws is a *photo ID* law or *non–photo ID* law. The difference being whether the law specifically mentions that the identification presented by the voter contain a photograph of the voter. Darker states in Figure 3.1 are those that ask voters for a photo ID while the lighter shaded states allow a broader range of identification, often any document with the voter's name and address. Unshaded states do not ask voters for any form of identification at the polls, requiring them to simply state their name and/or sign into the poll book. The second dimension addresses what happens to voters *without* acceptable ID. States marked with a star are commonly referred to as having "strict ID laws," voters without acceptable ID must cast a provisional ballot that is only counted if the individual returns to the board of election within a specified period after the election. If that voter is not able to produce acceptable ID, the provisional ballot is not counted; thus, having appropriate ID is *required* to cast a ballot. Other states with ID laws are generally referred to as non-strict laws. Here, provisions exist that allow poll workers to waive the ID requirements, often by having the voter sign an affidavit of identity, and allow the individual to cast a regular ballot that is counted without any additional actions taken by the voter. ID laws thus fall under one of four broad classifications: photo ID required, photo ID requested, non–photo ID required, non–photo ID requested.

Broadly speaking, the debate around ID laws centers on two main points. Proponents of ID laws maintain that they are necessary measures both to prevent fraud from altering the outcome of close elections and to protect voter confidence in the electoral system. As noted earlier, many Americans have concerns about the frequency of voter fraud. Research also suggests that a lack of confidence in electoral institutions might discourage some citizens from participating in elections (Norris, 2011). Critics argue that ID laws broadly, and photo ID laws specifically, as often a thinly disguised partisan attempt at election manipulation. Research suggests that there is little evidence that fraud is a problem in elections. By contrast, there is consistent evidence that millions lack access to photo ID and that these voters tend disproportionately to be racial and ethnic minorities, low-income, and younger voters (Pastor et al., 2010; Hershey, 2009; Baretto, Nuno, & Sanchez, 2007). Many of these groups are also key segments of the Democratic electoral coalition. Fowler (2006) finds that presidential elections often bring in many new and nonhabitual voters, who are more likely to be unaware of ID laws in place. Given which groups are known to lack access to photo ID, this presents a particular concern for the Democratic Party.

Republicans have nearly entirely driven the push to adopt ID requirements across the county (Hicks et al., 2014). Where Democrats lack the votes to block the adoption of ID laws they frequently turn to the courts to strike ID laws down. In many states, the legal challenges to ID laws are brought directly by the Democratic Party or closely allied groups (Wolf, 2014). Many federal courts have upheld ID laws in large part because there is little evidence that photo ID laws prevent individuals from voting. Surprisingly, research on the impact of voter ID laws on turnout continues to show mixed results. As the courts increasingly turn to empirical evidence to judge whether a disproportionate impact exists it is important to understand the impact of these laws on the American political system.

Advocacy groups are quick to point out that several segments of the population are less likely to have government-issued photo ID. The Brennan Center finds that low-income, minority, and older voters are less likely to have photo ID (Brennan Center, 2012). Among the most widely cited statistics is an ACLU estimate that 11 percent of all voters, roughly 21 million citizens, would be blocked from voting if photo ID requirements were in effect nationwide. The ACLU (2011) further estimates that as many as one in four African Americans would be disenfranchised under many strict photo ID requirements. Research on access to photo ID also shows that both minority and younger voters are less likely to have a government-issued photo ID, such as a driver's license (Pastor et al., 2010; Hershey, 2009; Baretto, Nuno, & Sanchez, 2009, 2007). Baretto, Nuno, and Sanchez (2009) find not only that stricter ID laws depress voter turnout, but also estimate that a number of U.S. House and Senate races would have switched outcomes, from Democratic victories to Republican victories, had photo ID requirements been in effect nationwide. Surprisingly, other research yields conflicting results.

One study of voter turnout in elections from 1996 to 2004 found that requiring voters to prove their identity at the polls was not associated with a drop in county-level turnout (Lott, 2006). Milyo (2007) examined turnout in Indiana before and after the passage of its photo ID law and saw no decline in voter turnout. Other researchers have also found little evidence that these laws harm turnout (Mycoff et al., 2009; Ansolabehere, 2009; Muhlhausen & Sikieh, 2007). These results would seem to confirm the opinion of the Supreme Court and other federal courts in 2008—that while requiring ID adds costs to the voting process, such costs are not "a substantial burden" to voting.

By contrast, other research appears to support the claim that these laws do in fact depress voter turnout in elections. Alvarez, Bailey, and Katz (2008), who examined elections from 2000 to 2006, found that stricter voter identification laws led to a decline in voter turnout, but find little evidence of any disproportionate impact on racial minorities. Vercellotti and Anderson (2006) find that the adoption of identification policies lowered turnout among some racial groups and younger voters in the 2004 presidential election. Others find evidence for a slight decline in turnout but no evidence of any disproportionate impact (Hood & Bullock, 2012; Erikson & Minnite, 2009). These mixed findings are especially surprising given the consistent finding that minority and low-income voters are less likely than whites to have acceptable photo ID.

Anecdotal evidence shows that many civic organizations are attempting to use photo ID laws to mobilize African American voters. Chong (1991) looks specifically at the civil rights movement of the 1950s and 1960s to show how a strong message is necessary to overcome the collective action problem inherent in the fight against discriminatory legal practices. As states strengthen identification requirements, numerous grassroots and national organizations have acted to mobilize the African American community to vote against those supporting these laws; in North Carolina (Fulton, 2016), Wisconsin (Issenberg, 2012), Texas (Melber, 2014), and Indiana (2008). Recent research has shown that ID laws are capable of incentivizing participation among core Democratic constituencies (Valentino & Nuener, 2017). The efforts of these groups likely complicate the attempt to find a consistent impact of voter identification on turnout, especially given that efforts are targeted at those groups thought to be most negatively impacted.

In large part, studies of voter turnout are driven by the costs associated with participation (Jackman, 1987; Riker & Ordeshook, 1968). State laws and elite activity can either increase these costs (e.g., through passage of restrictive laws) or help to alleviate these costs (e.g., through mobilization efforts). Elections in the United States are run by a patchwork of state laws that most often force voters to register well before Election Day and limit voting to one day during the week. Reforms often specifically target these costs in an effort to increase voter turnout. Referred collectively to convenience voting methods, many states have eased the process for obtaining an absentee ballot or allowing voters to visit a location and vote early. Five states have enacted laws that require a ballot to be mailed to all eligible voters in the state. Many of these reforms have met with strong Republican resistance, especially at the national level, due to concerns over election security.

The process of registering to vote has also been the target of significant reform. In 1993, the National Voter Registration Act (aka the motor voter law) was passed, which allows individuals to register to vote when renewing their driver's license. More recently, multiple states have moved to allow online voter registration or to allow for same-day voter registration. With the passage of these reforms many conclude that the legal barriers to voting have largely been removed (Gaimmo & Brox, 2010; Highton, 1997).

However, research on the impact of these laws does not show clear evidence that they improve voter turnout. Gronke, Galanes-Rosenbaum, and Miller (2007) find that the impact of many of these laws is negligible as they primarily impact individuals already committed to vote. This helps to retain current voters but does little to recruit new voters. Thus, the impact of increasing the costs of voting may fall primarily on those marginal voters debating whether or not to participate.

In this context, ID requirements are an explicit attempt to increase the costs of participation but may only prevent nonhabitual voters from participating. Researchers have long known that administrative barriers fall disproportionately on some segments of the population (Rosenstone & Wolfinger, 1978), but photo ID laws are thought to explicitly target core segments of the Democratic coalition (Baretto, Nuno, & Sanchez, 2007). Many of these groups have been the target of previous voting restrictions and maintain strong community organizations to advocate on their behalf, for example, the African American community. Although states that require photo ID make a free ID available to voters, obtaining this "free" ID can be costly in terms of time, money, and opportunity costs when individuals are required to bring specific, certified copies, of documentation to a government office prior to the election. Such costs are magnified when all of this must be done during normal business hours, which may not be full-time at many locations, unless the state opts to increase these.

The apparent threat to the viability of Democratic candidates provides a strong incentive for both the party and its allies to specifically target racial minorities for mobilization efforts. Many have already drawn parallels between photo ID requirements and Jim Crow–era poll taxes, and this image is often explicitly used to encourage urban minorities to have proper identification and get to the polls on Election Day. Efforts can be especially rewarding when many of these communities, especially African Americans, are known to vote overwhelmingly for Democratic candidates. Contrary to what many think, this provides an expectation that under certain circumstance restrictive laws can *increase* voter turnout. Voter photo ID laws present an opportunity for Democrats and allied organization to target key segments of their coalition with a message of attempted disenfranchisement, and often in a direct connection to the election of the first African American major-party candidate for president. Burden et al.'s (2014) analysis of early voting shows that election laws directly impact party electoral strategy, often leading to counterintuitive results.

This chapter takes a snapshot of the role of voter ID requirements during the 2016 U.S. presidential election to gauge their impact on turnout. Twenty-sixteen featured the first presidential election where a wide variety of ID laws were in effect, some for the first time. Given the expectation that presidential elections attract many nonhabitual voters, this might be expected to show the full impacts of ID laws. Presidential elections also attract more attention from local civic groups, which are those groups that anecdotal evidence suggests are doing the mobilization. The dependent variable for this analysis will be county voter turnout as a percentage of the voting age population. This provides the advantage of greater variation in the racial composition of areas where ID laws are in effect, as even homogenous states have pockets (often urban centers) of higher diversity. Within states, we expect mobilization efforts to be centered in areas with high concentrations of African Americans and other racial minorities, leading county turnout to be higher in these areas. Demographic information was taken from the U.S. Census Bureau's American Community Survey and used to control for factors commonly associated with voter turnout (Berinksy, 2005; Leighley, 1995). State-level controls are also used for the competitiveness of the presidential race, presence of other statewide offices on the ballot, and forms of convenience voting (taken from Gronke, Galanes-Rosenbaum, & Miller, 2007).

The main independent variables for this study are two dummy variables for the state's voter ID law in effect during 2016. Based on the NCSL coding procedure: Non-Photo ID is coded as 1 if the state requests or requires voters to present identification at the polls but does not require the ID to have a picture of the voter, Photo ID is coded as 1 if the state requests or requires voters to present identification at the polls and requires that ID to have a picture of the voter. For each measure, all states other states are coded as 0. States with no voter ID laws in effect during 2016 are coded as a 0 for both measures, this includes states that had adopted an ID law but did not have that law enforced due to court challenges or delayed implementation.

Table 3.1 reports the results of several models of the impact of voter ID laws on turnout during the 2016 elections. Results show that most

Table 3.1. State Voter ID Requirement and County Turnout in 2016

	Model 1	Model 2	Model 3	Model 4
Non-Photo ID Law	−0.449	2.144	2.400	2.603
	(2.344)	(2.090)	(2.072)	(2.083)
Photo ID Law	−0.183	2.925	3.429**	2.768–
	(2.228)	(1.836)	(1.833)	(1.843)
% African American Population		−0.057*	−0.003	−0.054*
		(0.026)	(0.011)	(0.026)
X Non-Photo ID Law		−0.010		−0.012
		(0.037)		(0.037)
X Photo ID Law		0.081**		0.081**
		(0.029)		(0.029)
% Hispanic Population		−0.095**	−0.114	−0.109**
		(0.014)	(0.026)	(0.026)
X Non-Photo ID Law			−0.042	−0.047
			(0.038)	(0.038)
X Photo ID Law			0.037	−0.034
			(0.028)	(0.029)
% High School Education		0.324**	0.332**	).326**
		(0.03)	(0.030)	(0.030)
Per Capita Income (in $1,000)		0.792**	0.781**	0.789**
		(0.032)	(0.032)	(0.032)
% Population Over 65		0.539**	0.544**	0.541**
		(0.031)	(0.031)	(0.031)

continued on next page

Table 3.1. Continued.

	Model 2	Model 3	Model 4
Presidential Election Win Margin	−0.159** (0.056)	−0.169** (0.055)	−0.161** (0.055)
No-Excuse Absentee Ballot	1.642 (2.414)	1.877 (2.383)	1.822 (2.383)
Early In-Person Voting	−1.413 (2.536)	−1.266 (2.542)	−1.278 (2.540)
All Elections by Mail	0.883 (3.496)	1.685 (3.443)	1.334 (3.443)
Same-Day Voter Registration	−0.640 (1.878)	−0.672 (1.852)	−0.677 (1.851)
U.S. Senate Election	−1.895 (1.716)	−1.982 (1.689)	−1.895 (1.689)
Gubernatorial Election	2.136 (1.871)	2.043 (1.841)	2.018 (1.841)
Constant	4.518 (3.271)	3.901 (3.258)	4.352 (3.257)
N	3,109	3,109	3,109

Note: Standard errors in parentheses, − = $P < .1$ * = $P < .05$ ** = $P < .01$

controls operate as expected; higher levels of education, age, and income correlate with higher county turnout on average and less competitive elections (i.e., higher *Presidential Election Win Margin*) feature lower turnout. The primary focus on this analysis is on the impact of the ID laws themselves and their interactions with county minority population, African American population in Model 2 and Hispanic population in Model 3. Model 4 then repeats the analysis including both interactions.

The top two rows in Table 3.1 estimate the overall impact of each type of ID on county turnout. One important factor to keep in mind is that this impact is conditioned by the minority population. For example, in Model 2 the presence of a voter ID law is interacted with county African American population. This means the impact of ID laws reported reflects the effect of ID laws on county turnout where the African American population is 0. To better assist in understanding the results, several figures have been generated using the estimates from Model 4.

Figure 3.2 visualizes the overall impact of voter ID laws on county turnout in 2016. While Model 4 estimates that photo ID requirements

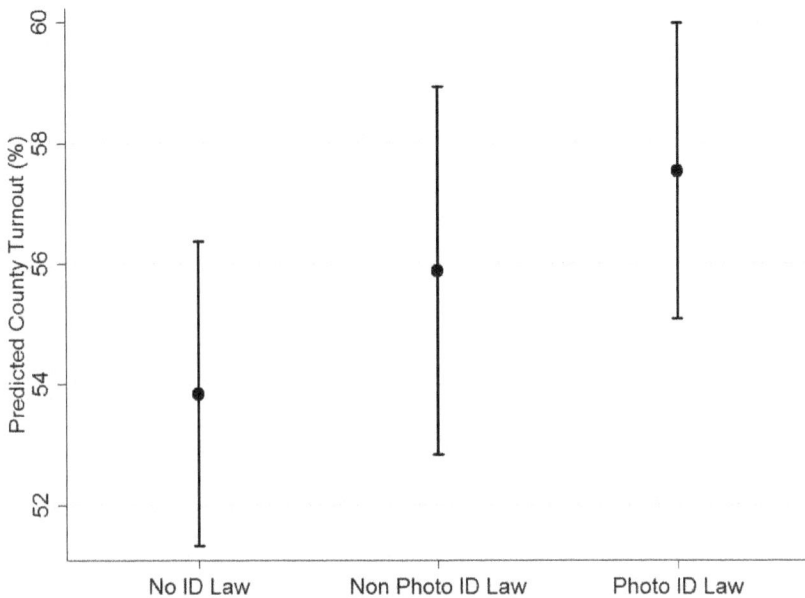

Figure 3.2. Predicted County Turnout.

increase turnout by roughly 2.7 percentage points, this impact is not significant at traditional levels. When estimating effects using the full model there is no significant impact from any form of ID requirement relative to counties where no ID law is in effect. This effect would be consistent with findings that many election laws have limited impact on new voters and primarily impact those most likely to participate. Note that other measures for convenience voting (no-excuse absentee, early in-person voting, etc.) are also estimated to have no significant impact on country turnout.

As for the impact on communities of color, we can see that ID laws do have a significant impact in highly African American counties. While the overall county African American population is, expectedly, negatively correlated with turnout, in states with a photo ID law in effect there is a significant *increase* in county turnout where there is a large African American population. These results are visualized in Figure 3.3, where the estimated impact of both non–photo ID and photo ID laws are compared to having no ID law in effect. The solid horizontal line indicates no difference in turnout between either non–photo ID or photo ID laws and no ID law. Where the associated confidence interval

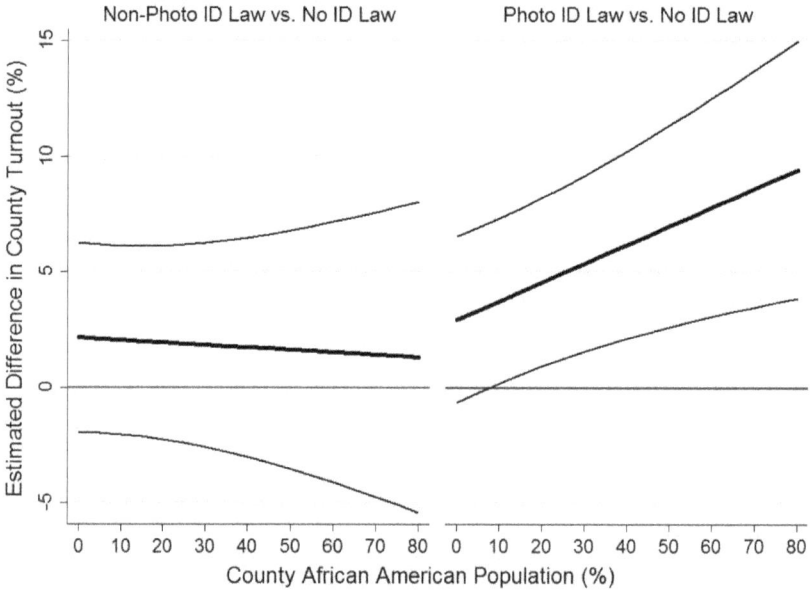

Figure 3.3. Estimated Differences in County Turnout.

lies completely above (or below), there is estimated to be significantly higher (or lower) turnout relative to similar counties with no ID law.

It is here that we see the positive impact of photo ID laws on voter turnout. While non–photo ID laws show no significant difference in turnout, counties with both a photo ID law in effect and large African American populations see an increase. For the current sample, the average county African American population is roughly 9 percent, at which level there is no difference in turnout. Counties then see a 1.2 percentage point increase in voter turnout for each standard deviation increase in the African American population (14.5 percent). The most heavily African American counties in 2016 saw a roughly nine point *higher* turnout than similar counties where photo ID laws were not in effect. This suggests something was occurring in these communities that was not happening in other counties with large African American populations that lacked a photo ID law.

One logical explanation for this impact is a possible backlash effect against voter photo ID laws. Laws requiring photo ID have generated a great deal of controversy and have become the face of the debate over requiring ID. Leading up to the 2016 elections, laws in multiple states were the subject of several legal challenges. Critics have been able to brand these laws as an attempt by Republican officials to create a "designer electorate" and local civic organizations are using this message to motivate African Americans to participate in elections. These appeals lack urgency in places where stringent ID laws are not in effect or are being actively debated. The African American community has historically seen many efforts to limit their participation in politics in general and voting in particular. These historical events spurred many community organizations that remain active in the fight to secure civil rights for African Americans, and these can easily be mobilized in response to a new perceived threat to voting rights.

In contrast, we can look at another group that many see as targeted by voter ID laws. Models 3 and 4 include interaction between ID laws and the county Hispanic population. Latinos have been subject to many of the same restrictions historically and continue to be underrepresented in American elections. Yet these communities often see fewer attempts at organization and mobilization relative to the African American community. While all models show a negative impact for the overall county Hispanic population, there is no significant impact on heavily Hispanic counties under either form of voter ID law. Note also that Model 3 does not include the interaction between African American population and voter ID laws, and this model shows an overall 3.4 percentage point increase in turnout associated with photo ID. This effect goes away once that interaction is returned in Model 4.

Together this shows some evidence that photo ID might be encouraging a backlash effect in some of the very communities thought to be most negatively impacted. While this might not be conclusive evidence, and does not test individual turnout specifically, it helps to place the effects of voter ID laws into the broader context of political parties using election law, as best they can, for an electoral advantage. This becomes increasingly relevant as courts continue to debate the constitutionality of these laws and whether they present an undue barrier to elections.

The Continuing Legal Fight over Photo ID Laws

The continued partisan division over photo ID requirements likely means that any major policy change is likely to come from the courts. To date, federal court have been willing to uphold ID requirements as a legitimate means for states to regulate elections. Two major precedents guide federal courts on election law: *Harper v Virginia* (1966), which requires both neutral application and a direct relationship to voting, and *Crawford v Marion County* (2008), which holds that photo ID laws meet these requirements when there is no evidence of a disproportionate impact on voting rates. Importantly, the *Crawford* decision also admitted that ID requirements increase barriers to voting for some eligible voters, opening another avenue for those seeking to challenge the law. Based on these guidelines, federal courts have been more hesitant to strike down ID laws unless there is clear evidence of intended racial bias in these laws, as has happened with North Carolina's photo ID requirement in 2016 and 2019.

State courts have proven more critical of photo ID requirements than their federal counterparts. State courts generally support the reasoning that ID requirements are reasonable considering the government's interest in maintaining voter confidence and preventing voter fraud. State lawyers often explicitly claim that ID laws are justified based on the need to "identify eligible voters at the polls" (*Martin v Kohls* [2014]; *Weinschenk v Missouri* [2006]). The Wisconsin Supreme Court explicitly held that photo ID requirements were a "reasonable regulation" for qualified voters during the election (*Milwaukee NAACP v Walker* [2014]). Even in states that have struck down photo ID requirements, such as Pennsylvania, judges have held that photo ID requirements are a "reasonable, non-discriminatory, non-severe" burden on the right to vote and have struck down laws for other reasons (Barnes, 2012).

One difference is often that state court judges are more critical of the link between preventing voter fraud and protecting voter confidence. For example, while the Wisconsin court upheld the state's photo ID law it also deferred to the state legislature on whether requiring ID was "the best way to preserve and protect the right to vote" (*Milwaukee NAACP v Walker* [2014], p. 6). Conversely, the Pennsylvania Commonwealth Court's decision striking down the state's photo ID requirement explicitly connected the interest in protecting voter confidence to evidence that fraud was a current, major problem in state elections. When the state could not effectively show that fraud was a problem, or that an ID requirement effectively combated this problem, the state's interest in using photo ID to protect voter confidence was limited.

A second difference is that state constitutions are often more explicit on protections of the right to vote than the U.S. Constitution. Where the U.S. Constitution provides several classes that cannot be denied the right to vote, state constitutions often provide positive protections on the right to vote generally. The constitutions of several states state that "no power, civil or military, shall at any time interfere to prevent the free exercise of the right of suffrage" (*Missouri Constitution* Art. I § 25; *Pennsylvania Constitution* Art. I § 5). State courts thus have the right to decide on how much of a burden states can place on voters before it interferes with a citizen's right to participate in elections. This rationale was used by the Pennsylvania Commonwealth Court to strike down a photo ID requirement in 2014, noting that while only a small number of voters lacked access to acceptable ID—roughly 430,000 out of the state's 13.7 million residents—the requirement still "inescapably . . . infring[ed] upon qualified elector's right to vote" (*Applewhite v Pennsylvania* [2014], p. 37). Additionally, some state constitutions lay out specific qualifications for voters in state elections, such as Arkansas, where voters must be a US. citizen, resident of Arkansas, 18 years old, and legally registered. The Arkansas Supreme Court thus struck down a photo ID requirement as an unconstitutional attempt to expand the requirements for voters (*Martin v Kohls* [2014]).

State courts have also been more receptive to the incidental costs that ID requirements place on voters. Several courts have used the lack of evidence surrounding concerns of voter fraud to shift emphasis to the difficulty voters face in acquiring acceptable ID. Stays on ID laws are often explicitly connected to concerns over whether citizens have the time to gain access to appropriate ID prior to the election. In Wisconsin, the decision upholding the state's photo ID law was not enforced due to the short time between when the decision was handed down (mid-July) and the November election. As part of their decision the Wisconsin Supreme Court also allowed state officials to issue voter ID cards without supplementary documents to both ease the process of obtaining ID and continue to ensure elections were "free" for all voters (*Milwaukee NAACP v Walker* [2014]). Pennsylvania judges placed a similar hold on the state's photo ID law as it worked through the legal system in the months prior to the 2012 presidential election. Judges would later focus specifically on both the difficulty of obtaining photo ID and the state's efforts to educate voters about the requirement when striking down the law (AP, 2014; *Applewhite v Pennsylvania* [2014]). Missouri judges directly tied the costs of documents needed to obtain the free photo ID card made available by the state to a limitation on the right to vote when striking down that state's photo ID requirement (*Weinschenk v Missouri* [2006]).

While these arguments have largely featured primarily is state courts, they have begun to play a role in recent federal decisions on voter ID requirements. While *Crawford* remains the controlling federal precedent, it did not close the door on issues regarding access to ID. Federal judges have begun looking at these additional costs, monetary and otherwise, in their decisions regarding constitutionality of photo ID requirements. In the summer of 2016 numerous decisions on voter photo ID requirements were made in federal courts, with laws in several states being placed on hold. The very next election cycle featured a new round of cases, with a photo ID law in North Dakota being blocked and later reinstated by federal courts. To date the U.S. Supreme Court has not taken up any cases reviewing the overall constitutionality of ID laws.

Voter ID and the Future of American Elections

Requiring ID at the polls remains a contentious issue in American politics. Since the 2016 election several states have changed ID laws. Arkansas, Iowa, and West Virginia have created new ID requirements, a photo ID and non–photo ID laws respectively, North Dakota and Texas have strengthened existing requirements. Laws in both Arkansas and Texas represent attempts to replace earlier laws that were struck down by either the state supreme court or federal courts. Thus, it appears that courts are likely to remain key actors in the debate surrounding the necessity and constitutionality of ID requirements.

As the American electorate continues to grow more diverse, concerns over access to acceptable ID will feature heavily in the debate given the potential for these laws to disenfranchise racial minorities. While the evidence on the impact of these laws on turnout is mixed, there are a few key takeaways to be aware of. First, the adoption of ID laws appears to be a strategic act by the Republican Party. The idea that a political party will use election laws to its advantage is not a new idea and we often see both major parties push election reforms they believe will benefit them. Hicks et al. (2014) note that the best predictor of the adoption of an ID law is not just Republican Party control, but also the competitiveness of elections. North Carolina has become a key swing state in presidential elections and features multiple high-profile court cases regarding photo ID. Additionally, North Dakota in 2018 featured a key U.S. Senate race, Wisconsin has featured multiple close statewide races, and Texas's potential move toward competitiveness as the Hispanic population increases. This casts doubt on the motives behind laws that, while seemingly neutral and broadly popular, were adopted without a single Democratic vote.

Related to this are the consistent findings that while isolated incidents of fraud can be found, there is no reason to believe it is widespread or a major threat to the integrity of elections. Still, many voters may perceive fraud as being more common and desire steps to prevent it. This introduces a large amount of subjectivity into any discussion on the necessity of ID requirements.

Second, there is room for concern regarding access to ID cards. While *Crawford* points out that driver's license are now a fundamental part of American life, access to them is not universal. Studies consistently point out that certain segments of the population, notably racial and ethnic minorities, are less likely to have access to government-issued photo ID. Laws in both North Carolina and Texas were struck down in recent years over these very concerns. States that require photo ID to vote do make free voter ID cards available, but these often entail both monetary (to acquire certified copies of needed documents) and opportunity (to get to the DMV during business hours) costs to potential voters. As courts increasingly turn to considerations of these costs, the future of ID laws is far from certain.

As many of these groups thought to be most impacted are also key segments of the Democratic coalition, this provides strong incentives to the Democratic Party to resist the adoption of ID requirements and mobilize voters when it cannot. As both parties become increasingly polarized along racial lines the risks and rewards of ID laws increase for each party.

The intersection of these two facts often complicates any analysis of the impact of these laws on voter turnout. Many of these laws have only been in effect for a relatively short period of time, for instance, the number of strict photo ID laws doubled from 2012 to 2016. These laws also target segments of the population that already vote at lower rates, and groups that have seen multiple historical attempts to limit their participation in elections. Groups like the NAACP are active in not just filing legal challenges to ID laws, but also mobilizing the African American community in response to these laws.

Evidence from this chapter shows that these efforts may be paying off. Looking at a snapshot of county turnout during the 2016 election we see that ID laws do not appear to have had a negative impact on average turnout rates. Instead, we see evidence that counties with both photo ID laws *and* large proportions of African Americans see a significant increase in voter turnout. This effect appears to be present in counties with higher than average African American populations, the very place a strategic, coordinated attempt to mobilize in response to these laws would be taking place. Combined with anecdotal evidence from states where these laws are actively debated, it appears that, rather than acting as a barrier to minority participation, ID laws are encouraging a backlash effect that may be negating their most sinister intent.

References

ACLU. (2011). Oppose voter identification legislation: Fact sheet. American Civil Liberties Union. July 21.
Adler, B. (2008). Young activists mobilize against ID law. *Politico*. January 21.
Alvarez, M, Bailey, D., & Katz, J. (2008). The effects of voter identification laws on turnout. California Institute of Technology Working Paper (1267R).
Alvarez, M., Ansolabehere, S., Berinsky, A., Lenz, G., Stewart III, C., & Hall, T. (2009). 2008 Survey of the performance of American elections. Caltech/MIT Voting Technology Project.
Ansolabehere, S. (2009). Effects of identification requirements on voting: Evidence from the experiences of voters on election day. *PS: Political Science & Politics, 42*, 127–130.
Applewhite v. Commonwealth of Pennsylvania 71 MAP (2012).
Baretto, M., Nuno, S., & Sanchez, G. (2007). Voter ID requirements and the disenfranchisement of Latino, Black, and Asian voters. Annual Meeting of the American Political Science Association, Chicago, Illinois. vol. 30.
Berinksy, A. (2005). The perverse consequences of electoral reform in the United States. *American Politics Research, 33*, 471–491.
Biggers, D., & Hanmer, M. (2011). Annual Meeting of the Midwestern Political Science Association, Chicago, Illinois. Web.
Burden, B., Canon, D., Mayer, K., & Moynihan, D. (2014). Election laws, mobilization, and turnout: The unanticipated consequences of election reform." *American Journal of Political Science, 58*, 95–109.
Bush v. Gore 531 US 98 (2000).
Chong, D. (1991). *Collective action and the civil rights movement*. University of Chicago Press.
Crawford v. Marion County Election Board 553 US 181 (2008).
Erikson, R., & Minnite, L. (2009). Modeling problems in the voter identification–voter turnout debate. *Election Law Journal, 8*, 85–101.

Fowler, J. (2006). Habitual voting and behavioral turnout. *The Journal of Politics*, 68, 335–344.

Fulton, D. (2016). Inspiring mobilization "like never before," NC voter ID law goes on trial. *Common Dreams*, January 25.

Giammo, J., & Brox, B. (2010). Reducing the costs of participation: Are states getting a return on early voting? *Political Research Quarterly*, 63, 295–303.

Gronke, P., Galanes-Rosenbaum, E., & Miller, P. (2007). Early voting and turnout. *PS: Political Science and Politics*, 40, 639–645.

Harper v. Virginia State Board of Elections 383 US 663 (1966).

Hershey, M. (2009). What we know about voter-ID laws, registration, and turnout. *PS: Political Science and Politics*, 42, 87–91.

Hicks, W., McKee, S., Sellers, M., & Smith, D. (2015). A principle or a strategy? Voter identification laws and partisan competition in the American states. *Political Research Quarterly*, 68, 18–33.

Highton, B. (1997). Easy registration and voter turnout. *The Journal of Politics*, 59, 565–575.

Hood, M. V. III, & Bullock III, C. (2012). "Much ado about nothing? An empirical assessment of the Georgia voter identification statute. *State Politics and Policy Quarterly*, 12, 394–414.

Issenberg, S. (2014). Don't let them disenfranchise you: Can Democratic organizers use voter ID laws to mobilize outraged supporters? *Slate*. September 28.

Jackman, R. (1987). Political institutions and voter turnout in the industrial democracies. *The American Political Science Review*, 81, 405–423.

Keyssar, A. (2000). *The right to vote: The contested history of democracy in the United States*. Basic Books.

Leighley, J. (1995). Attitudes, opportunities, and incentives: A field essay on political participation. *Political Research Quarterly*, 48, 181–209.

Lott, J. (2006). Evidence of voter fraud and the impact that regulations to reduce fraud have on voter participation rates. SSRN 925611.

Marley, P., & Stein, J. (2016). Court ruling softens Wisconsin voter ID law. *Milwaukee Journal Sentinel*. April 13.

Martin v. Kohls 2014 Ark. 427 (2014).

McDonald, M. (2010). American voter turnout in historical perspective. In J. Leighly (Ed.), *The Oxford handbook of American elections and political behavior*. Oxford University Press.

Melber, A. (2014). As Texas votes early, Voter ID sparks frustration and motivation. MSNBC. October 29.

Milwaukee Branch of the NAACP v. Walker 2012 AP001652 (2014).

Milyo, J. (2007). The effects of photographic identification on voter turnout in Indiana: A county-level analysis. *Institute of Public Policy, University of Missouri, Report 10-2007*.

Minnite, L. (2010). *The myth of voter fraud*. Cornell University Press.

Muhlhausen, D., & Sikich, K. (2007). New analysis shows voter identification laws do not reduce turnout. Heritage Center for Data Analysis. September 10.

Mycoff, J., Wagner, M., & Wilson, D. (2007). The empirical effects of voter-ID laws: Present or absent? *PS: Political Science and Politics, 42,* 121–126.

National Conference of State Legislatures. (2017). History of voter ID. May 31.

National Conference of State Legislatures. (2016). Voter identification requirements: Voter ID laws. October 31.

Norris, P. (2011). *Democratic deficit: Critical citizens revisited.* Cambridge University Press.

Pastor, R., Santos, R., Prevost, A., & Stoilov, V. (2010). Voting and ID requirements: A survey of registered voters in three states. *American Review of Public Administration, 40,* 461–481.

Pear, R. (2002). Congress passes bill to clean up electoral system. *The New York Times.* October 17.

Posner, R. (2013). I did not "recant" on voter ID laws. *New Republic.* October 27.

Riker, W., & Ordeshook, P. (1968). A theory of the calculus of voting. *American Political Science Review, 62,* 25–42.

Rosenstone, S., & Wolfinger, R. (1978). The effect of registration laws on voter turnout. *American Political Science Review, 72,* 22–45.

Urbina, I. (2008). Voter ID laws are set to face crucial test. *The New York Times.* January 7.

Valentino, N., & Neuner, F. (2017). Why the sky didn't fall: Mobilizing anger in reaction to voter ID laws. *Political Psychology, 38,* 331–350.

Weinshenk v. Missouri VR-MO-0061 (2006).

Wolf, R. (2014). Supreme Court blocks Wisconsin's voter ID law. *USA Today.* October 9.

Chapter 4

Backlash!

Do Restrictive Voting Laws Mobilize Their Opponents?

Michael A. Smith

Introduction: A Gaffe in Pennsylvania

Voter ID, which is gonna allow Governor Romney to win the state of Pennsylvania—done.

—Pennsylvania House Majority Leader
Mike Turazi (R-Marshall Township), 2012

In 2012, shortly before the presidential election, Republican majorities in the Pennsylvania house and senate passed a new voter ID law. In and of itself, there was nothing particularly remarkable about this—as noted in earlier chapters, such laws had become fairly common by this time. However, each state's restrictive voting laws bear a unique signature. In the case of Pennsylvania's law, a few peculiarities were evident. First, the law was set to take effect almost immediately after passing. Signed by Gov. Tom Corbett in March 2012, the law was supposed to be in effect by the November general elections. Many other states include a longer period including an ensuing election before such laws take effect.

Even more startling were the Pennsylvania House majority leader's comments about the new law, which open this chapter. As documented in previous chapters of this book, the case for these restrictive new laws typically centers on fraud prevention. Yet shortly after the Keystone State passed its new law, Representative Mike Turzai famously made these comments at a state Republican meeting (Weinger, 2012).

This was an extremely unusual way to describe such a law. Because it offered what appeared to be a naked, partisan rationale, the quote went viral and was bandied about the blogosphere, particularly by Democrats working to provoke a backlash. Democrats gleefully seized on the talking point that Turzai's quote constituted an acknowledgment that the purpose of voter ID laws was to elect Republicans by suppressing Democratic voters. Of course, Democrats and their supporters argued that all such laws had this same purpose, suppressing Democratic-leaning constituencies. As far as they were concerned, Turazi had committed a classic gaffe. *Gaffe* is a term famously defined by political commentator Michael Kinsley as "when a politician tells the truth—some obvious truth he isn't supposed to say."

For Democrats and liberals, Turazi had indiscreetly spilled the beans about the true purpose of the laws. Liberal blogs such as the *Huffington Post* labeled this quote as the first well-publicized, public mention by a Republican official in any state that the laws were designed to change electoral outcomes, not control fraud (Johnson, 2012).

There were two possible benefits that voter ID law opponents could cull from Turazi's stumble. The first concerned pending lawsuits regarding the laws. Turazi's quote was the first public pronouncement by a voter ID law supporter stating that the laws had a partisan intent, which could cast the laws under greater legal scrutiny. Indeed, the Pennsylvania law would soon be embroiled in a series of back-and-forth court rulings that left that state's voters baffled on Election Day. However, the Turazi quote also provided powerful new fuel to an evolving new strategy Democrats could use regarding the laws. Regardless of whether or not they and their allies on this issue could get the laws overturned, the laws offered new political opportunities. Why not capitalize on the opportunity by integrating a new message into Get Out the Vote (GOTV) drives. Roughly summarized, that message was, "The Republicans are trying to take away your vote. Don't let them get away with it. Vote this November."

Of course, this must be taken with a grain of salt. The kinds of political blogs and cable TV shows that publicize gaffes like Turzai's are primarily consumed by those who are already frequent voters (and frequent Democratic voters). Yet, the Turzai incident had the kind of viral quality that spreads beyond the usual "political junkies" to some in the general public, particularly if it is being retold during phone bank calls and door-to-door visits by Democratic GOTV Volunteers.

In 2012, Pennsylvania was a unique case for another reason as well. The rushed, last-minute law did not survive the numerous court challenges in time to be fully in effect on Election Day. Instead, the last court ruling before the election left the state's voters in a strange situation. The judge who ruled on the case did not believe that he had the authority to overturn the provisions that allowed poll workers to request that voters show ID. However, the judge did rule that voters were not required to *show* the ID. Thus, Pennsylvania was the only state in which poll workers could, at their discretion, request voter ID but the voters were not required to present it—a truly confusing state of affairs.

Using data from the Inter-University Consortium of Political and Social Research (ICPSR) at the University of Michigan, it appears that voters contacted by political campaigns were more likely to vote in Pennsylvania than they were in other states, once other factors such as political competitiveness were taken into account. Turazi's inflammatory quote certainly offers a plausible explanation for the evident backlash effect in the Keystone State: one that fits well with Daniel Biggers's (2014) research hypothesis that "backlash" messages are more powerful than some others as a GOTV tool.

Is There a Backlash Effect Outside Pennsylvania?

Is there a voter backlash against the new, more restrictive laws, one that is actually boosting turnout? Beyond Pennsylvania, earlier research was inconclusive. However, Nichols (2014) notes that African American turnout remained stable in 2012 compared to 2008, while turnout numbers among others dropped. With African American voters frequently perceived as one of the targets of these new laws, and most of them strongly in support of President Obama, one cannot help but speculate about a possible backlash that would explain why African American turnout bucked the trend of dropping turnout in 2012. Nichols reports anecdotal evidence of African American organizers being told by voters that they were mobilized by their anger at these laws—but such anecdotal evidence is hardly definitive.

Other odd results include the huge increase in turnout, particularly for Democrats, in the Tampa Bay, Florida, area in 2012 relative to 2008. Florida was one of the states passing a bevy of restrictive new voting laws in time for the 2012 elections, as well as the site of the 2012 Republican National Convention. Some of these laws cut the days for early voting. For example, there was an attempt to eliminate Sunday early voting, which was often used by African American church pastors and community organizers as an opportunity to organize voter drives called "souls to the polls" or "golden week." In practice, the Florida laws were ambiguous and the limitations on early voting were not applied evenly in each county. Tampa saw long lines of early voters that stretched for hours in some precincts—yet turnout, particularly for Democrats, spiked in Tampa (Smith, Anderson, & Rackaway, 2012). Our subsequent research (Smith, Rackaway, & Anderson, 2014) found that restrictions on early voting actually correlate with higher voter turnout and Democratic vote share, controlling for other factors such as electoral competitiveness of a state, circumstantial yet fascinating evidence of a possible backlash.

Biggers (2014) conducted an elaborate, experimental project that involved two different types of get-out-the-vote mailings to low-propensity voters. One mailer featured a "backlash message," something along the lines of "don't let them take your right to vote away." The control group mailer featured a different, more generic, nonbacklash message about the value of voting. Biggers found that the backlash mailer might have produced stronger reactions in voters than did the other message, lending further credence to the case for a backlash effect. However, his results were inconclusive.

Searching for Evidence: Back to Basics

Data limitations may account for the difficulties that Biggers had finding statistically significant outcomes, and this is true of our own 2014 paper as well. Biggers conducted a "field experiment" in which he created his own campaign mailings with different messages: an experimental group with a pro-backlash GOTV message, and a control group with a more generic message. He then measured voter turnout rates among the two groups receiving the mailings and compared the rates for those receiving the backlash message with those for the group receiving the generic message. His findings of a relationship were too small to reach statistical significance, thus his research was inconclusive.

This chapter takes an alternative approach, analyzing panel data from the ICPSR at the University of Michigan. Panel data results from respondents who agreed to be contacted repeatedly for follow-up questions. Panel data is incredibly useful for political science research, but it also has limitations. Perhaps the biggest such limitation is that many respondents do not agree to this, thus those that do create a smaller dataset. The smaller the dataset, the harder it is to draw generalizations, especially when breaking the numbers down even further, for example, state by state.

A second problem with panel data is that it exacerbates a problem that exists with all election surveys, called oversampling. While modern day voter turnout in U.S. presidential elections is between 50 and 60 percent of the voting-eligible population, turnout among survey respondents is well over 70 percent and often much higher. Put simply, those who are not interested in voting tend also to refuse to answer surveys about voting. A related problem is those who report voting even though they did not do so, because they do not want to be embarrassed. However, that second problem can be corrected by verifying voter turnout with local election authorities.

Today's election forecasting polls also adjust the results using a procedure called multivariate analysis with post-stratification ("Mr. P," for short), in which "weights" are added to the data for certain demographic groups that are underrepresented (Smith, 2017). Even more powerful is the methodology of *New York Times* blogger and forecaster extraordinaire Nate Silver, who delivers remarkably accurate forecasts by averaging multiple polls, using a formula that he keeps proprietary. Vindicated yet again, Silver repeatedly stated that "Donald Trump has a path to the Presidency" in 2016, while most others assumed a Hillary Clinton victory.

Even in this era of cell phones and declining landline use, strategies such as "Mr. P" and Silver's poll averaging still work fine for predicting overall election results, but when it comes to breaking down the how and why of voting behavior, even small inaccuracies in poll samples can give political scientists fits. One recent example is particularly relevant to this book: using the Congressional Cooperative Election Studies (CCEP) conducted online by YouGov, Jesse Richman, Gulshan Chattha, and David Earnest (2014) argue that they have stumbled upon evidence that noncitizens vote in U.S. elections, creating something of a stir in conservative media outlets. Yet Stephen Ansolabehere, Samantha Luks, and Bryan Schaffner (2014) counter that Richman et al.'s results are simply the result of small amounts of measurement error in a huge dataset. This is particularly noteworthy, because Ansolabehere, Luks, and Shaffner are directly responsible for administering the CCES studies—essentially, the administrators of the studies themselves are arguing that Richman et al. are misusing the data. Not surprisingly, Richman and colleagues have a response, arguing that there is indeed still some evidence for noncitizen voting, and the debate continues (2017). In 2018, both Richman and Ansolabehere were summoned to appear in Kansas, serving as expert witnesses for opposing sides in the *Fish v Kobach* case regarding the state's proof-of-citizenship law (Lowry, 2018). The federal court ruled against the law.

Data, Methods, and Results

The hypothesis of this paper is that a voter's propensity to vote may actually be higher if there is a combination of having been mobilized, and residing in a state with a restrictive new law. The argument is, if the voter lives in a state with such a new law and if a political campaign capitalizes on that by increasing or changing the tone of its get-out-the-vote efforts, the voter would in fact be more likely to vote than if neither of these conditions existed. Because Democratic-leaning constituencies are often perceived to be the targets of such laws, we also check for an increased likelihood of voting for Obama under these circumstances.

To test for the evidence of a backlash, this paper features two models using the 2012 panel data from the National Elections Studies conducted by the Inter-University Consortium for Political and Social Research at the University of Michigan. The method used is *probit analysis,* which is a variation of the classic multivariate regression model used with a dependent variable that has only two categories. Independent control variables come from a classic Rosenstone and Wolfinger (1978) study of the impact of voting laws and control variables on voter turnout. They are

- Respondent's level of education
- Respondent's level of education, squared

- Respondent's age
- Respondent's age, squared
- Region in which the respondent lives (Northeast, North Central, South, or West)

The relationships between education and voting, and age and voting, respectively, are well documented. Inputting the education variable squared is intuitive, because the impact of rising education levels may "level off" or even slightly reverse itself once one moves beyond the bachelor's degree. Likewise, while citizens are generally more likely to vote as they get older, voters who are a good deal older might be less likely to vote due to mobility or other issues, so it is intuitive to also square this data. The dependent variable is whether or not the respondent voted. Turnout varies in different regions of the country, and has for years, so this, too, makes sense as a control variable.

Independent variables of interest include:

- Whether or not the respondent lives in a state that passed any of the following laws between the 2008 and 2012 elections, excluding those that were enjoined by court rulings, as described by the Brennan Center (2012):
    o Laws allowing poll workers to request, but not require photo ID (Pennsylvania)
    o Laws requiring photo ID (Kansas, New Hampshire, Virginia, Tennessee)
    o Laws making it more difficult to restore voting rights after a felony conviction (Iowa, South Dakota, Tennessee)
    o Laws making it more difficult to register to vote (Florida, Illinois, Texas, Tennessee, Wisconsin)
    o Laws limiting early voting (Florida, Georgia)
- Whether or not the respondent was contacted by anyone to ask them to vote
- The interaction of the respondent contact variable with each of the variables measuring residence in a state that had restrictive new laws in effect

Variables about race and Hispanic/Latino origin were not used because of a large number of missing cases in the dataset.

Table 4.1 summarizes results from the first model using whether or not the respondent voted as the dependent variable. Among the control variables, education and age correlate strongly and positively with voting,

Table 4.1. Dependent Variable: Whether or Not the Respondent Voted

	Estimate	Std. Error	t value	Pr(>|t|)
Intercept^	2.967e-02	7.014e-02	0.423	0.67232
Education level	4.144e-02	3.724e-03	11.126	<2e-16***
Education level squared	-4.002e-04	3.678e-05	-10.879	<2e-16***
Age	1.017e-02	2.559e-03	3.976	7.21e-05***
Age squared	-5.545e-05	2.534e-05	-2.188	0.02873*
Region: Northeast^	-1.581e-02	2.692e-02	-0.587	0.55702
Region: North Central^	1.937e-02	2.320e-02	0.835	0.40384
Region: South^	-1.061e-03	2.277e-02	-0.047	0.96283
Was R contacted?	4.825e-02	1.800e-02	2.681	0.00740**
R live in state **requesting** photo ID?	-4.566e-02	6.011e-02	-0.760	0.44760
R live in state **requiring** photo ID?	-6.923e-02	6.248e-02	-1.108	0.26802
R live in state complicating voting after felony?	1.473e-01	6.003e-02	2.454	0.01421*
R live in state complicating voter registration?	-1.444e-02	2.875e-02	-0.502	0.61547
R live in a state restricting early voting?	-6.927e-03	4.160e-02	-0.167	0.86777
ID Request*Contacted	1.862e-01	7.144e-02	2.606	0.00922**
PhotoID*Contacted	5.366e-04	8.160e-02	0.007	0.99475
Restore after felony* Contacted	-1.183e-01	8.973e-02	-1.319	0.18737
Registration complication* Contacted	2.400e-02	3.935e-02	0.610	0.54189
Restricted early voting* Contacted	1.798e-03	5.471e-02	0.033	0.97378

^The "default" region is West.

Signif. codes: 0 '***' 0.001 '**' 0.01 '*' 0.05 '.' 01 ' ' 1 but education and age *squared* correlate *negatively* with voting, as predicted. What this means is that older age and higher levels of education do mean a greater likelihood of voting, but this relationship declines or even reverses at very high levels of each (holding a graduate degree or being more than 80 years old, for example). Region was not significant.

As to the variables of interest, there is a clear link between the voter's being contacted and her being more likely to vote. Of course, correlation does not cause causation—it may be that those already intending to vote are also being contacted by campaigns, or perhaps mobilization is at work, or it may be a combination. At any rate, the correlation between the two variables is clear.

With regard to the stand-alone variables measuring restrictive new state voting laws, a puzzle we discovered in earlier research—with completely different data (Smith, Rackaway, & Anderson, 2014)—reasserts itself yet again: the respondent is more likely to vote in the states that passed new restrictions on voting after a felony conviction. Two of the three states to which this applies are famously high-turnout states (Iowa and South Dakota)—but it is a puzzle that the "North Central" region variable did not control this effect. If indeed voters are more likely to vote when such laws pass, it is for now a matter of speculation as to why, but one possible explanation is that voters have more confidence in the system when these controls on those with a criminal past are present. Iowa's new law, for example, requires that any fines and restitution handed down as part of a sentence be paid in full before voting rights will be restored—this may increase confidence that the system is not allowing some people to take advantage, specifically unfair advantage, by voting before they have paid their debt to society. This remains speculation, however.

What lies at the core of this chapter are the variables combining voter contact with restrictive laws. If there is a backlash effect in this data, then the combination variables should show positive correlation with whether or not the respondents voted. In fact, the backlash effect does materialize—but only for one combination: laws allowing poll workers the discretion to request ID, combined with the voter being contacted.

The only state to which this applies is Pennsylvania, so the political climate of that state in 2012 deserves mention. Unfortunately, since the new-laws variables are measured at the state level, and this one applies to only one state, it is impossible to rule out other factors which might explain why 2012 voter turnout was higher among Pennsylvanians in our sample than would otherwise be predicted by our model. It is true that the Romney campaign tried a last-minute "push" in Pennsylvania that was unsuccessful in delivering that state's electoral votes. Yet Pennsylvania's situation regarding voter ID laws is also a likely suspect for this result.

Pennsylvania's voter ID laws in 2012 were—to put it kindly—a mess. The state General Assembly had passed a new bill requiring photo IDs for voting. However, the law had been enjoined by court rulings and could not be enforced in 2012. Judge Robert Simpson of Commonwealth (State) Court ruled that the state had not done enough to "ensure liberal access" to the photo ID cards. Instead, he ruled that poll workers could request a photo ID but if the voter did not have one, s/he could still vote on a normal voting machine: a provisional ballot was unnecessary. As things stood, the state's voters entered Election Day confused about whether or not they needed a photo ID to vote (Bronner, 2012).

Furthermore, backlash might indeed have been fueled by the publicity surrounding this particular law—specifically, the Turazi quote mentioned earlier in this chapter (Johnson, 2012). No other evidence of the backlash effect is evident in our model, but the Pennsylvania results are noteworthy.

Table 4.2 summarizes results for a second model, this one addressing whether or not the respondent cast a ballot for Obama as the dependent variable. Results here are unremarkable, but for a few things. Among the control variables, the finding for voters in the South is counterintuitive, given the modern-day South's strong preference for Republican presidential candidates. In our model, living in the South correlates with being more likely to vote for Obama. This may seem surprising until one realizes that we were unable to input race into our model due to missing data—the South's large African American population helps explain the result, particularly because the other variables included may soak up the tendency of Southern whites to vote heavily Republican today. More intuitive is the strong link between a voter's having been contacted, and her having voted for Obama: Democrats are well known for investing in GOTV campaigns, particularly since Obama's 2008 campaign (Sides & Vavreck, 2014). As before, the correlation-not-causation problem rears its head: it is not clear if these voter contacts in fact influenced the voters to favor Obama or if, instead, those likely to favor Obama were simply more likely to be contacted.

Interestingly, there are no significant relationships between voting for Obama and any of our voting law variables, nor among our variables combining voting law changes with the voter's having been contacted.

Table 4.2. Dependent Variable: Whether the Respondent Voted for Obama

	Estimate	Std. Error	t value	Pr(>|t|)
Intercept^	5.491e-01	1.115e-01	4.924	9.19e-07***
Education level	−6.577e-03	5.740e-03	−1.146	0.252000
Education level squared	5.886e-05	5.686e-05	1.035	0.300737
Age	4.017e-03	3.947e-03	1.018	0.308916
Age squared	−6.081e-05	3.833e-05	−1.587	0.112782
Region: Northeast^	2.614e-02	4.000e-02	0.653	0.513547
Region: North Central^	4.022e-03	3.472e-02	0.116	0.907769
Region: South^	9.240e-02	3.454e-02	2.675	0.007531**
Was R contacted?	9.452e-02	2.695e-02	3.507	0.000464***
R live in state **requesting** photo ID?	−9.625e-02	9.291e-02	−1.036	0.300357
R live in state **requiring** photo ID?	−1.207e-01	9.421e-02	−1.281	0.200257
R live in state complicating voting after felony?	−4.287e-02	8.862e-02	−0.484	0.628663
R live in state complicating voter registration?	−4.221e-02	4.422e-02	−0.955	0.339915
R live in a state restricting early voting?	2.839e-04	6.444e-02	0.004	0.996485
ID Request*Contacted	1.655e-01	1.068e-01	1.549	0.121458
Photo ID*Contacted	5.290e-02	1.231e-01	0.430	0.667362
Restore after felony* Contacted	−1.111e-01	1.312e-01	−0.847	0.397090
Registration complication* Contacted	2.264e-02	5.973e-02	0.379	0.704687
Restricted early voting* Contacted	−1.469e-01	8.318e-02	−1.765	0.077653

^The "default" region is West.
Signif. codes: 0 '***' 0.001 '**' 0.01 '*' 0.05 '.' 01 ' ' 1

The ID Request*Contacted combined variable, for example, produces a coefficient in the expected direction (more likely to vote for Obama) but falling short of the conventional thresholds for statistical significance.

Conclusion

The evidence of a backlash effect is present, but not overwhelming, in this model. The impact on propensity to vote among the Pennsylvanians in our sample is noteworthy and intuitive, given Representative Turzai's notable gaffe. Pennsylvania's confused voting laws, the state's political competitiveness, and Turzai's seeming admission that the laws were designed to affect the election, appear to have been the perfect storm for a small but significant backlash effect. However, it is harder to trace any actual change in partisan outcomes to this phenomenon. Perhaps most telling is that Turzai's prediction was famously incorrect: Pennsylvanians chose Barack Obama over Mitt Romney by 52 to 47 percent in 2012, down from 54–44 percent in the 2008 Obama-McCain race and largely mirroring national trends. Our earlier research was more nuanced regarding the new voting laws themselves—there, we found a small but significant effect when new restrictions on registration are combined with poverty: as poverty rises, voter turnout drops faster in states that passed these sorts of laws than it does elsewhere. While this new study does not find independent, vote-suppressing impacts of the new laws, it does support a larger, overall conclusion earlier research: whether in the form of vote suppression or backlash, it is easier to track effects of the laws on turnout than it is to show that they alter the partisan composition of the electorate. This finding harks all the way back to the classic Rosenstone and Wolfinger piece from 1978. Back then, they were studying new laws such as same-day voter registration designed to boost turnout, whereas critics claim that these newer laws were designed to suppress it. Yet, while Wolfinger and Rosenstone found that more-liberal registration laws might boost turnout by several percentage points, they and others subsequently found far less evidence that such changes would affect electoral outcomes. Interestingly, this also applies to the backlash effect: it is easier to document that it might affect turnout, increasing it in one state. It is far more difficult to show that it changes election results.

References

Ansolabehere, S., Luks, S., & Schaffner, B. (2014). The perils of cherry picking low frequency events in large sample surveys. Cooperative Congressional Election Study. November 5.

Arizona v. Inter Tribal Council of Arizona, Inc. 570 U.S. 1 (2013).
Berman, A. (2011). The GOP war on voting. *Rolling Stone*. August 30.
Bennion, E. (2005). Caught in the ground wars: Mobilizing voters during a competitive congressional campaign. *Annals of the American Academy of Political and Social Science, 601*, 123–141.
Biggers, D. (2014). Can the backlash against voter ID laws mobilize low-propensity voters? A field experiment examining the effect on political participation of efforts to restrict Democratic rights? Paper Presented to the Midwest Political Science Association Annual Meetings.
Brennan Center for Justice. (2012). Voting laws roundup: 2012. New York University School of Law.
Bronner, E. (2012). Voter ID rules fail tests across country. *New York Times*. October 2.
Colby, D. (1986). The Voting Rights Act and Black registration in Mississippi. *Publius, 16*, 123–137.
Crawford v. Marion County Election Board. 553 U.S. 181 (2008).
Fish v. Kobach, 189 F. Supp. 3d 1107 (D. Kan. 2016).
Fullerton, A., & Borch, C. (2008). Reconsidering explanations for regional convergence in voter registration and turnout in the United States, 1956–2000. *Sociological Forum, 23*, 755–785.
Gaskins, K., & Iyer, S. (2012). The challenge of obtaining voter identification. New York University Brennan Center for Justice. July 18.
Highton, B., & Wolfinger, R. (1998). Estimating effects of the National Voter Registration Act of 1993. *Political Behavior, 20*, 79–104.
Jackson, R. (2003). Differential influences on Latino electoral participation. *Political Behavior, 25*, 339–366.
Johnson, L. (2012). Mike Turzai, Pennsylvania GOP House Majority Leader: Voter ID will allow Mitt Romney to win state. *Huffington Post*. June 20.
King, J. (1994). Political culture, registration laws, and voter turnout among the American states. *Publius, 24*, 115–127.
Knack, S. (1995). Does motor voter work? Evidence from state-level data. *Journal of Politics, 57*, 796–811.
Knack, S., & White, J. (2000). Election-day registration and turnout inequality. *Political Behavior, 22*, 29–44.
Kobach, K. (2011). The case for voter ID. *Wall Street Journal*. May 23.
Lipton, E., & Urbina, I. (2007). In 5-year effort, scant evidence of voter fraud. *The New York Times*. April 12.
Lowry, B. (2018). His own witness doesn't back Kobach claims that illegal votes cost Trump popular vote. *Kansas City Star*. March 13.
McDonald, M. (2008). Portable voter registration. *Political Behavior, 30*: 491–501.
Michelson, M. (2005). Meeting the challenge of Latino voter mobilization. *Annals of American Academy of Political and Social Science, 601*, 85–101.

Mitchell, G., & Wlezien, C. (1995). The impact of legal constraints on voter registration, turnout, and the composition of the American electorate. *Political Behavior, 17*, 179–202.

Nagler, J. (1991). The effect of registration laws and education on U.S. voter turnout. *American Political Science Review, 85*, 1393–1405.

National Conference of State Legislators. (2014). Voter identification requirements | Voter ID laws.

Nichols, J. (2013). How voter backlash against voter suppression is changing our politics. *The Nation*. April 29.

Oliver, J., & Wolfinger, R. (1999). Jury aversion and voter registration. *American Political Science Review, 93*, 147–152.

Priest, C. (2015). Dual registration voting systems: Safer and fairer? *Stanford Law Review Online*. January 25.

Richman, J., Chattha, G., & Earnest, D. (2014). Do non-citizens vote U.S. elections? *Electoral Studies, 36*, 149–157.

Richman, J., Chattha, G., & Earnest, D. (2017). A valid analysis of a small subsample. Working Paper. Old Dominion University.

Rosenstone, S., & Wolfinger, R. (1978). The effect of registration laws on voter turnout. *American Political Science Review, 72*, 22–45.

Schur, L., Shields, T. Kruse, D., & Schriner, K. (2002). Enabling democracy: Disability and voter turnout. *Political Research Quarterly, 55.* 167–190.

Shelby County v. Holder 570 U.S. 529. (2013).

Sides, J., & Vavrek, L. (2013). *The gamble: Choice and chance in the 2012 presidential election*. Princeton University Press.

Simpson, D. (2010). Picturing democracy: An empirical analysis of the impact on voter turnout of photographic voter identification requirements in Georgia. Doctoral Dissertation, Georgia College and State University.

Smith, M. (2013). Kobach's voter-fraud claims don't hold up. *Wichita Eagle*. October 27.

Smith, M. (2017). Polling for the 2016 presidential election: What went wrong? Midwest Political Science Association Blog. January 11.

Smith, M., Anderson, K., & Chapman Rackaway, C. (2012). Was the vote suppressed in 2012? A tentative look at the impact of voter-suppression laws in the 2012 presidential election. Paper presented to the Northeastern Political Science Association Annual Meetings.

Smith, M., Rackaway, C., & Anderson, K. (2014). *State voting laws in America: Historical statutes and their modern implications*. Palgrave Pivot.

Vedlitz, A. (1985). Registration drives and Black voting in the South. *Journal of Politics, 47*, 643–651.

Weinger, M. (2012). Mike Turzai: Voter ID helps GOP win state. Politico.com. June 25.

Zarnow, Z., & Shay, C. (2012). Free but no liberty: How Florida contravenes the Voting Rights Act by preventing persons previously convicted of felonies from voting. *National Lawyer's Review Guild*. v. 69.

Chapter 5

Using Cross-Sectional, Time Series, and Border Effects to Identify the Impact of Restrictive Voting Laws

Bekah Selby and Michael A. Smith

Introduction

A wave of restrictive new voting laws passed after the 2000 general election. According to Minnite (2014) and Levitt (2007), much of the initial enthusiasm for these restrictive laws centered around the city of St. Louis, Missouri. St. Louis's heavy voter turnout played a key role in the posthumous election of Gov. Mel Carnahan (D) over incumbent U.S. Senator John Ashcroft (R), with Carnahan's widow Jean being appointed to serve in the Senate seat. St. Louis is an independent city separated from St. Louis County before the Civil War, with its own election board. By 2000, the city featured poorly organized election procedures including outdated voter rolls and long lines. Voters in line before the polls closed were allowed to vote, even though they did not actually cast ballots until after closing, due to the waiting times. Last-minute decisions and court rulings were involved. Missouri's other senator at the time, Christopher "Kit" Bond (R) called for crackdowns on voter fraud, but Minnite's and Levitt's analyses indicated that, if anything, St. Louis's disorganized procedure led to fewer, not more ballots being cast that night in this heavily Democratic city.

Of course, 2000's photo-finish vote tally and protracted recount in Florida also fueled this drive. The Help America Vote Act (HAVA) of 2003 was passed in response to concerns about the way in which the balloting was conducted, particularly in Florida and Missouri. HAVA offered grants to the states for updating election equipment. Some states and counties used this money to purchase electronic voting machines that do not use paper ballots, leading to further controversy (Greenmeier, 2008). However, new voting equipment was not the only provision. Based in part on the recommendations of the Carter-Baker commission, HAVA also mandated that states require some sort of identification at the polls. State legislatures' responses to this law varied widely, with a distinct partisan cast. Some states mandated simply that voters verify their identity when registering to vote (Underhill, 2018). Others required that verification occur when voting for the first time. At the other extreme, some states passed restrictive new laws including a mandate that voters prove their American citizenship when registering to vote (Kansas, Arizona, Alabama, Georgia), and/or restrictive ID laws requiring a state-issued photo ID (Kansas, Wisconsin, Indiana). Still other states passed "soft" ID laws that allowed for provisional balloting or for non-photo ID, but the implementation of such laws still drew lawsuits and critics, for example in Texas. A few states had such restrictions in place for the 2012 presidential election (Obama-Romney), but far more took effect by 2016 (Trump-Clinton). In some cases, this was because the laws were not set to take effect until after 2012, while in others, court challenges were still ongoing in 2012 but resolved, at least tentatively, by 2016. In still other states, the court challenges continue (Brennan Center, 2018). The U.S. Supreme Court upheld Indiana's strict Photo ID law in *Crawford v Marion County Election Board* (2008), but that ruling turned on certain specifics of the law's implementation, such as the state's outreach efforts encouraging voters without drivers' licenses to get free ID cards. As a result, *Crawford* did not bring an end to the other lawsuits.

Finally, some states responded to the HAVA mandate with a grab bag of new restrictions on voting. For example, early voting, which began shortly before HAVA, was restricted in presidential "battleground" states such as Ohio and North Carolina, with critics charging that the rollback was meant to limit or end so-called Golden Week or Souls to the Polls drives, in which predominantly African American church congregations spearheaded drives to cast early ballots on the Sunday before election day. In fact, Mataconis (2014) found that minority voters were more likely than whites to participate in early voting. South Dakota and Iowa made it more difficult for former felons to restore their voting rights after serving their sentences (Brennan Center, 2012). Other states, such as Florida, made it more difficult to conduct voter registration drives, after a 2009 conservative-led controversy regarding registration canvasses by the liberal interest group ACORN, now defunct.

A clear, partisan trend has emerged during this century. Heavily Democratic states have maintained or advanced procedures to ease voter registration and balloting. No state exemplifies this better than Oregon, which implemented vote-by-mail procedures in 2000 and then followed up with European-style automatic voter registration in 2016. Washington and Colorado also feature voting by mail, while California is now implementing automatic registration. These are joined by several states in the northern tier of the country—not all of them heavily Democratic—which have continued to follow their 1970s-era laws providing for same-day voter registration (some only on Election Day, some all the time). These include Minnesota and New Hampshire. Despite other new restrictions in Wisconsin, Election Day registration remains in place there as well. North Dakota does not require registration at all. Other innovations include pre-registration of 16 and 17 year-olds, implemented in Massachusetts and, for a time, in North Carolina.

By contrast, the restrictive new laws such as photo ID mandates, proof of citizenship for registration, and restriction on early voting and those convicted of felonies tend to be seen in "battleground" states with GOP-majority legislatures. Critics allege that restrictive new laws passed in states like Wisconsin, Ohio, Pennsylvania, North Carolina, Arizona, Georgia, and Florida are designed to "flip" these states' electoral voters from Democratic to Republican, or to prevent them from flipping in the other direction. At times, Republican legislative leaders have even made gaffes in which they, in effect, have validated these worries (Blake, 2016). Texas also features such laws. While the state remains solidly in Republican hands, speculation abounds that the state's increasingly urban and Hispanic population will one day make it "Blue," fueling concerns that the restrictive laws may be designed to thwart such a shift.

One state that stands out here is Kansas. Heavily Republican, the Kansas Legislature's passage of a particularly restrictive set of laws in 2011 does not fit the pattern. Heavily Republican neighbors Nebraska and Oklahoma have not passed such restrictions, and there is little risk that any of these Plains states will turn Democratic-voting Blue in the near future. However, Kansas is the home of Kris Kobach, the advocate and author of such laws for his own state and many others. He served as secretary of state from 2010–18, and Kobach had also been an advocate for these laws beforehand, helping to draft them in Arizona and Alabama. Kobach first stepped onto the national stage with a strongly anti–illegal immigrant set of viewpoints. He had a hand in drafting Arizona's controversial "show your papers" law as well as its proof-of-citizenship law, which is similar to the one he convinced the Kansas Legislature to pass upon being elected secretary of state (Smith, Rackaway, & Anderson, 2014). The Arizona proof of citizenship law was declared, in part, to be unconstitutional by the U.S. Supreme Court in *Arizona v Inter Tribal Council* (2013). Undaunted, Kobach claimed that proof-of-citizenship and photo ID laws are needed to prevent undocumented immigrants from voting, despite the paucity of evidence for this claim. In response to the *Inter Tribal Council* ruling, Kobach continues to push for amendments to the National Voter Registration Act (NVRA, or "Motor Voter") of 1993, which would allow states to ask voters for such proof on the federal registration form (Lowry & Woodall, 2017). However, Kansas's proof-of-citizenship law was overturned by the federal courts in *Fish v Kobach* (2018).

The claim that undocumented immigrants register and vote serves as a key justification for many of these laws, and is widely assailed by critics. Thus, much of the most-cited research in this field concerns the rationale for the laws rather than their impact. Numerous scholars, include Minnite and Levitt, have shown that voter fraud in the modern-day United States is extraordinarily rare. One study that bucks the trend is Richman, Chattha, and Earnest (2014), which finds cases of noncitizen registration and voting based on the Comparative Congressional Election Studies (CCES). However, CCES organizers Ansolabehere, Luks, and Schaffner (2015) reject the inferences that Richman et al. are drawing from the studies that Ansolabehere et al. administer. According to these critics, Richman and colleagues are cherry-picking low-frequency events from a large dataset. Analysis of multiyear panel data indicates that the events of noncitizen registration and voting are almost certainly due to response error, not actual noncitizen participation in U.S. elections.

The bigger challenge lies in documenting the impact of the laws themselves. Regardless of whether or not they are necessary, are these laws dampening turnout? Are they suppressing Democratic voters, as critics allege? Alvarez, Bailey, and Katz (2011) used a Bayesian shrinkage estimator to project that the impact of Photo ID laws is approximately 2 percent lower turnout—enough to sway the outcome of a close election. However, such a shift would require a heavy partisan bias. Yet few of the newer studies have reversed the earlier findings of Rosenstone and

Wolfinger (1978). In that classic study, the authors concluded that ease or difficulty of registering and voting can shift turnout by a few percentage points, but it has little impact on the composition of the electorate or on partisan outcomes. Applied to the more recent developments, this conclusion suggests that while the new photo ID, proof-of-citizenship, and other restrictions may lower turnout a bit, their impact is not confined to Democratic-leaning constituencies. Instead, the restrictions affect other groups and Republican voters as well.

Variables

To test these claims, the authors constructed a series of regression-based models, which utilize county-level data. The models feature these variables:

DEPENDENT VARIABLES (ALL BY COUNTY)

- Republican vote share (of total votes cast, 2012 and 2016, from Politico.com)
- Democratic vote share (as above)
- Other vote share (as above, total for all third-party and independent candidates)
- Turnout (all presidential votes as percentage of adult population, as per U.S. Census county population estimates from the previous year and percentage of adult population from the last decennial census).

INDEPENDENT VARIABLES BEING STUDIED

- "Soft" ID laws—new law requiring ID to vote which either allows a provisional ballot to be cast if the voter does not have ID, or allows non-photo ID such as a utility bill with the voter's name and address, taking effect in time for either the 2012 or 2016 elections, respectively.
- ID laws—new law strictly requiring state-issued photo ID for voting, taking effect in 2012 or 2016, respectively.
- Proof-of-citizenship law—new law requiring proof of citizenship, taking effect in 2016 (Kansas only—Arizona's was

stayed and overturned by court rulings, while Alabama and Georgia never implemented theirs due to the same)

INDEPENDENT CONTROL VARIABLES (ALL DATA IS FROM THE 2010 U.S. CENSUS, BY COUNTY)

- % Black
- % Other race
- % in various age groups (see tables)
- % Unemployment
- Per capita income

Empirical Specifications and Analysis

To identify the causal impact of voter restriction laws, we exploit the timing in enactment of laws. This is done using variants of a fixed effects, generalized differences-in-differences empirical model.

$$Y_{ct} = \beta_0 + \beta_1 ID_{ct} + \beta_2 SoftID_{ct} + \beta_3 Proof_{ct} + \beta_4 Other_{ct} + \Gamma X_{ct} + \delta_t + \alpha_s + \Omega_s t + u_{ct}$$

The variable Y is the Republican share of the vote, Democratic share, third-party share, or voter turnout; *ID*, *Soft ID*, *Proof*, and *Other* take on the value of one when county c is in a state which has the given law enacted in year t and is zero otherwise; X is a matrix of control variables for demographics and economic conditions; δ and α are year and state (s) fixed effects; Ω is state specific time trends; and, u_{ct} is an independently and identically distributed error term.

Tables 5.1–5.4 report the results of this analysis. Column 1 only includes controls, Column 2 adds the fixed effects dummies, and Column 3 includes regression results allowing the mean of the dependent variable to have a state-specific time trend. The interpretation of the coefficient depends on the specification. The coefficient in Column 1 should be interpreted as the difference in mean Y in states with a restriction law in effect relative to states with no law in effect, all of the control variables held constant. The coefficient in Column 2 should be interpreted as the difference in mean Y in states with a restriction law in effect relative to states with no law in effect, allowing for this mean to vary within each state/year pair, assuming states have common trends. Lastly, the coefficient in Column 3 should be interpreted as before but the mean can have a time trend and allows this trend to differ by state.

Another specification looks at the individual impact of the laws within state:

$$Y_{ct} = \beta_0 + \beta_1 L_{ct} + \Gamma X_{ct} + \delta_t + \alpha_s + u_{ct}$$

Where everything is defined as above except for L which takes on the value of one in county c in year t when either ID, SoftID, Proof, or Other is enacted, and is zero otherwise. The data are restricted to only states that pass this type of law, so the coefficient is interpreted as the impact of the laws relative to periods before enactment within state. Tables 5.5–5.8 report the estimates for this model.

The third specification investigates whether there was a difference in impact by the timing of the laws.

$$Y_{ct} = \beta_0 + \beta_1 L2012_{ct} + \beta_2 L2016_{ct} + \Gamma X_{ct} + \delta_t + \alpha_s + u_{ct}$$

Where L2012 is a law passed between 2008–12 and equals 1 for each voting year it is enacted and zero otherwise, L2016 is a law passed between 2012–16 and equals 1 for each voting year it is enacted and zero otherwise.

The final specification investigates the border effect:

$$Y_{ct} = \beta_0 + \beta_1 L_{ct} + \beta_2 B_c + \beta_3 (L_{ct} * B_c) + \Gamma X_{ct} + \delta_t + \alpha_s + u_{ct}$$

Where B is an indicator taking on the value of 1 if the county is a border county. This is a differences in difference specification where the control group are counties in states with no law and are not border counties. β_3 is the differences in differences estimator and the linear combination $\beta_1 + \beta_3$ gives the difference in expected means of states which pass a law and are on a border from states that have no law and are on the border.

Results

Overall, the analysis indicates that ID laws dampen turnout in the cross-state comparisons, while Soft ID laws dampen turnout in the within-county, time series analysis. The findings may be driven by the availability of data. Far more states had these ID and soft ID laws take effect during the time period, thus producing a larger number of cases and better estimates. At the other end of the extreme, research on proof-of-citizenship laws is highly tentative because there was only one state with such laws in effect during the time period (Kansas). The impact of proof-of-citizenship laws over time is well worth studying, particularly if court rulings and/or acts of Congress allow those laws to be implemented in other states. However, that may not be the case given the *Fish v Kobach* ruling against the Kansas law, which occurred after the time period studied here. The findings for strict ID laws (coded simply as "ID" in the tables) pointed to lower turnout in the models that featured controls for fixed effects, and for both fixed effects and state trends, respectively. Likewise, ID laws correlated with lower turnout in the model for within-county change over time. Thus, this analysis gives substantial reason to believe that strict ID laws also lower turnout.

In sum, the results summarized on Table 5.9 indicate that a strict ID law implemented 2012–16 correlates with a turnout that is about 4 percent lower, while such laws implemented in 2008–12 are not significant. Soft ID laws correlate with turnout nearly 2 percent lower if implemented 2008–12, and nearly 2.5 percent lower if implemented 2012–16. The results for Democratic, Republican, and Other vote share vary based on model specification, and many are insignificant.

Much like Rosenstone and Wolfinger's findings for registration laws, these models indicate that restrictive laws (ID and Soft ID, in this case) lower turnout by a few percentage points, but without much change in the composition of the electorate. More research is needed, particularly for proof of citizenship laws, which currently occur in too few cases for strong conclusions to be reached. Yet the findings for ID and Soft ID laws are significant, they hold up across models, and they confirm the hypothesis that such laws correlate with lower turnout. However, they do not substantiate the argument that the laws appreciably shift the composition of the electorate toward being less Democratic.

Table 5.1. Effect of Independent Variables on Republican Share of Vote

	(1) REPSHARE	(2) REPSHARE	(3) REPSHARE
ID	2.080	−0.909	0.628
	(3.346)	(1.207)	(0.946)
SOFT ID	3.399**	−2.087	−1.505
	(1.679)	(1.296)	(0.949)
Proof of Citizenship	4.591	−1.334	−0.766
	(3.416)	(1.160)	(1.754)
Other Law	2.748	1.457	0.480
	(2.590)	(0.963)	(1.255)
% Black	−0.325***	−0.622***	−0.621***
	(0.0527)	(0.0655)	(0.0669)
% Other Race	−0.514***	−0.430***	−0.421***
	(0.0850)	(0.0809)	(0.0818)
% < 14 years old	1.626***	0.934***	0.893***
	(0.240)	(0.295)	(0.297)
% 15–19 years old	−1.133*	−0.0200	−0.0105
	(0.667)	(0.358)	(0.356)
% 30–39 years old	0.631	0.112	0.0685
	(0.395)	(0.221)	(0.217)
% 40–59 years old	−0.290	0.596**	0.651**
	(0.321)	(0.243)	(0.245)
% 60 and older	0.944***	0.651***	0.636***
	(0.186)	(0.134)	(0.137)
Unemployment Rate	−1.129***	−1.070**	−1.101**
	(0.364)	(0.414)	(0.451)
Per Capita Income (1000s)	−0.290***	−0.187***	−0.194***
	(0.0686)	(0.0632)	(0.0616)
N	8315	8315	8315
adj. R-sq	0.357	0.652	0.665
Controls	Yes	Yes	Yes
Fixed Effects		Yes	Yes
State Trends			Yes

Standard errors in parentheses clustered at state level.

* $p < 0.10$ ** $p < 0.05$ *** $p < 0.01$

Table 5.2. Effect of Independent Variables on Democratic Share of Vote

	(1) DEMSHARE	(2) DEMSHARE	(3) DEMSHARE
ID	−2.247	1.771	0.484
	(3.041)	(1.515)	(1.123)
SOFT ID	−2.915*	3.301**	2.664*
	(1.583)	(1.422)	(1.332)
Proof of Citizenship	−5.676*	0.775	1.909
	(3.153)	(1.259)	(1.858)
Other Law	−2.620	−1.062	−0.537
	(2.513)	(0.985)	(1.484)
% Black	0.358***	0.644***	0.642***
	(0.0526)	(0.0655)	(0.0671)
% Other Race	0.498***	0.436***	0.427***
	(0.0798)	(0.0826)	(0.0832)
% < 14 years old	−1.598***	−0.890***	−0.829***
	(0.264)	(0.301)	(0.297)
% 15–19 years old	1.000	−0.163	−0.0318
	(0.663)	(0.351)	(0.343)
% 30–39 years old	−1.042**	−0.245	−0.0470
	(0.415)	(0.214)	(0.212)
% 40–59 years old	0.548	−0.585**	−0.647**
	(0.339)	(0.243)	(0.245)
% 60 and older	−1.099***	−0.655***	−0.581***
	(0.195)	(0.127)	(0.129)
Unemployment Rate	1.254***	1.047**	1.111**
	(0.346)	(0.424)	(0.461)
Per Capita Income (1000s)	0.269***	0.188***	0.198***
	(0.0669)	(0.0620)	(0.0605)
N	8315	8315	8315
adj. R-sq	0.397	0.678	0.691
Controls	Yes	Yes	Yes
Fixed Effects		Yes	Yes
State Trends			Yes

Standard errors in parentheses clustered at state level.

* $p < 0.10$ ** $p < 0.05$ *** $p < 0.01$

Table 5.3. Effect of Independent Variables on Independent/3rd Party Share of Vote

	(1) OTHSHARE	(2) OTHSHARE	(3) OTHSHARE
ID	0.168	–0.861	–1.112
	(0.435)	(0.558)	(0.706)
SOFT ID	–0.485*	–1.214***	–1.159
	(0.261)	(0.395)	(0.745)
Proof of Citizenship	1.085*	0.558	–1.143
	(0.557)	(0.390)	(0.969)
Other Law	–0.129	–0.394	0.0574
	(0.327)	(0.261)	(0.471)
% Black	–0.0333***	–0.0222***	–0.0215***
	(0.00459)	(0.00218)	(0.00191)
% Other Race	0.0160	–0.00631	–0.00617
	(0.0137)	(0.00475)	(0.00486)
% < 14 years old	–0.0282	–0.0435***	–0.0638***
	(0.0572)	(0.0126)	(0.00752)
% 15–19 years old	0.133	0.183***	0.0423
	(0.128)	(0.0595)	(0.0260)
% 30–39 years old	0.411***	0.133***	–0.0214
	(0.118)	(0.0418)	(0.0373)
% 40–59 years old	–0.258***	–0.0109	–0.00375
	(0.0437)	(0.0152)	(0.0105)
% 60 and older	0.155***	0.00420	–0.0548***
	(0.0525)	(0.0154)	(0.0178)
Unemployment Rate	–0.125***	0.0238	–0.0101
	(0.0389)	(0.0341)	(0.0240)
Per Capita Income (1000s)	0.0206***	–0.000119	–0.00427
	(0.00646)	(0.00403)	(0.00328)
N	8315	8315	8315
adj. R-sq	0.264	0.652	0.773
Controls	Yes	Yes	Yes
Fixed Effects		Yes	Yes
State Trends			Yes

Standard errors in parentheses clustered at state level.

* $p < 0.10$ ** $p < 0.05$ *** $p < 0.01$

Table 5.4. Effect of Independent Variables on Turnout

	(1) TURNOUT	(2) TURNOUT	(3) TURNOUT
ID	−2.616	−3.130***	−3.641*
	(2.40)	(0.81)	(1.83)
SOFT ID	−6.130***	0.519	0.419
	(1.01)	(0.87)	(2.32)
Proof of Citizenship	−1.301	2.712***	0.507
	(2.28)	(0.55)	(2.20)
Other Law	−1.409	0.893	0.876
	(1.76)	(0.60)	(1.03)
% Black	0.113***	0.102***	0.107***
	(0.04)	(0.02)	(0.02)
% Other Race	−0.0847	−0.0794***	−0.0708***
	(0.06)	(0.03)	(0.03)
% < 14 years old	0.555***	0.469***	0.444***
	(0.20)	(0.12)	(0.11)
% 15–19 years old	1.796***	1.450***	1.402***
	(0.37)	(0.27)	(0.27)
% 30–39 years old	−0.919***	−0.765***	−0.825***
	(0.25)	(0.23)	(0.25)
% 40–59 years old	1.365***	1.109***	1.123***
	(0.11)	(0.09)	(0.09)
% 60 and older	0.715***	0.657***	0.645***
	(0.10)	(0.10)	(0.10)
Unemployment Rate	−0.734***	−0.562***	−0.682***
	(0.18)	(0.12)	(0.13)
Per Capita Income (1000s)	0.269***	0.287***	0.279***
	(0.05)	(0.04)	(0.04)
N	8315	8315	8315
adj. R-sq	0.338	0.54	0.55
Controls	Yes	Yes	Yes
Fixed Effects		Yes	Yes
State Trends			Yes

Standard errors in parentheses clustered at state level.
* $p < 0.10$ ** $p < 0.05$ *** $p < 0.01$

Table 5.5. Effect of Independent Variables on Republican Share of Vote (Focus Only on One Law)

	(1) REPSHARE	(2) REPSHARE	(3) REPSHARE	(4) REPSHARE
ID	0.572 (0.625)			
SOFT ID		−0.960 (1.161)		
Proof of Citizenship			0.864 (.)	
Other Law				1.237 (1.554)
% Black	−0.625*** (0.0951)	−0.252 (0.303)	−0.853 (.)	−0.531*** (0.134)
% Other Race	−0.413*** (0.102)	−1.783** (0.514)	−0.794 (.)	−0.224 (0.136)
% < 14 years old	0.957** (0.326)	−0.121 (0.207)	1.501 (.)	0.526 (0.379)
% 15–19 years old	1.931* (0.414)	0.0856 (0.367)	0.575 (.)	0.312 (0.467)
% 30–39 years old	0.337* (0.161)	0.830*** (0.172)	0.356 (.)	0.514** (0.222)
% 40–59 years old	0.685 (0.353)	1.446*** (0.151)	−0.182 (.)	0.969** (0.307)
% 60 and older	0.916** (0.267)	0.686** (0.166)	1.270 (.)	0.908*** (0.115)
Unemployment Rate	−1.276*** (0.302)	−2.572* (1.051)	−2.076 (.)	−1.902** (0.745)
Per Capita Income (1000s)	−0.128 (0.149)	0.135 (0.0808)	0.0803 (.)	−0.0553 (0.103)
N	1350	1146	315	3317
adj. R-sq	0.817	0.561	0.705	0.596
Controls	Yes	Yes	Yes	Yes
Fixed Effects	Yes	Yes	Yes	Yes

Standard errors in parentheses clustered at state level.

* $p < 0.10$ ** $p < 0.05$ *** $p < 0.01$

Table 5.6. Effect of Independent Variables on Democratic Share of Vote (Focus Only on One Law)

	(1) DEMSHARE	(2) DEMSHARE	(3) DEMSHARE	(4) DEMSHARE
ID	−0.119 (0.613)			
SOFT ID		1.230 (1.093)		
Proof of Citizenship			−4.887 (.)	
Other Law				−1.265 (1.814)
% Black	0.646*** (0.0959)	0.274 (0.305)	0.871 (.)	0.550*** (0.136)
% Other Race	0.437*** (0.0961)	1.690** (0.526)	0.794 (.)	0.229 (0.140)
% < 14 years old	−0.925** (0.301)	0.175 (0.205)	−1.386 (.)	−0.472 (0.384)
% 15–19 years old	−1.106** (0.433)	−0.111 (0.384)	−0.520 (.)	−0.373 (0.477)
% 30–39 years old	−0.479* (0.213)	0.855*** (0.180)	−0.395 (.)	−0.565** (0.235)
% 40–59 years old	−0.634 (0.355)	−1.439*** (0.148)	0.169 (.)	−0.960** (0.307)
% 60 and older	−0.925** (0.263)	−0.663** (0.167)	−1.210 (.)	−0.879*** (0.112)
Unemployment Rate	1.191*** (0.287)	2.627* (1.063)	2.005 (.)	1.923** (0.798)
Per Capita Income (1000s)	0.114 (0.144)	−0.129 (0.0815)	−0.0628 (.)	0.0574 (0.100)
N	1350	1146	315	3317
adj. R-sq	0.836	0.567	0.735	0.611
Controls	Yes	Yes	Yes	Yes
Fixed Effects	Yes	Yes	Yes	Yes

Standard errors in parentheses clustered at state level.
* $p < 0.10$ ** $p < 0.05$ *** $p < 0.01$

Table 5.7. Effect of Independent Variables on Independent/3rd Party Share of Vote (Focus Only on One Law)

	(1) OTHSHARE	(2) OTHSHARE	(3) OTHSHARE	(4) OTHSHARE
ID	−0.453 (0.318)			
SOFT ID		−0.270** (0.0828)		
Proof of Citizenship			4.023 (.)	
Other Law				0.0282 (0.340)
% Black	−0.0214*** (0.00185)	−0.0222*** (0.00261)	−0.0185 (.)	−0.0186*** (0.00234)
% Other Race	−0.0243*** (0.00655)	0.0930** (0.0273)	0.000466 (.)	−0.00555 (0.00591)
% < 14 years old	−0.0322 (0.0274)	−0.0546*** (0.00545)	−0.116 (.)	−0.0538*** (0.00956)
% 15–19 years old	1.175*** (0.0429)	0.0259 (0.0189)	−0.0551 (.)	0.0615* (0.0284)
% 30–39 years old	0.142* (0.0694)	0.0252* (0.0109)	0.0385 (.)	0.0503** (0.0162)
% 40–59 years old	−0.0509* (0.0250)	−0.00703 (0.00843)	0.0134 (.)	−0.00863 (0.00801)
% 60 and older	0.00911 (0.0160)	−0.0232*** (0.000919)	−0.0595 (.)	−0.0286*** (0.00628)
Unemployment Rate	0.0857** (0.0293)	−0.0553** (0.0148)	0.0712 (.)	−0.0218 (0.0573)
Per Capita Income (1000s)	0.0140 (0.00883)	−0.00583 (0.00327)	−0.0175 (.)	−0.00206 (0.00616)
N	1350	1146	315	3317
adj. R-sq	0.742	0.723	0.839	0.763
Controls	Yes	Yes	Yes	Yes
Fixed Effects	Yes	Yes	Yes	Yes

Standard errors in parentheses clustered at state level.

* $p < 0.10$ ** $p < 0.05$ *** $p < 0.01$

Table 5.8. Effect of Independent Variables on Turnout (Focus Only on One Law)

	(1) TURNOUT	(2) TURNOUT	(3) TURNOUT	(4) TURNOUT
ID	−3.365** (1.231)			
SOFT ID		−2.204*** (0.402)		
Proof of Citizenship			−7.061 (.)	
Other Law				0.318 (1.018)
% Black	0.117*** (0.00812)	0.0932 (0.0819)	−0.272 (.)	0.0877*** (0.0194)
% Other Race	−0.110** (0.0421)	0.692** (0.246)	−0.195 (.)	−0.0241 (0.0338)
% < 14 years old	0.343 (0.302)	0.326*** (0.0605)	−0.266 (.)	0.481** (0.189)
% 15–19 years old	1.703** (0.482)	0.899** (0.238)	1.053 (.)	1.755*** (0.464)
% 30–39 years old	−0.469 (0.407)	−1.518*** (0.182)	0.726 (.)	−0.433 (0.399)
% 40–59 years old	1.042*** (0.168)	1.313** (0.295)	0.611 (.)	1.212*** (0.121)
% 60 and older	0.728*** (0.178)	0.768*** (0.0577)	0.944 (.)	0.806*** (0.135)
Unemployment Rate	0.0317 (0.282)	−0.209 (0.175)	0.173 (.)	−0.467*** (0.109)
Per Capita Income (1000s)	0.446*** (0.0592)	0.288*** (0.0481)	0.262 (.)	0.355*** (0.0521)
N	1350	1146	315	3317
adj. R-sq	0.458	0.510	0.614	0.671
Controls	Yes	Yes	Yes	Yes
Fixed Effects	Yes	Yes	Yes	Yes

Standard errors in parentheses clustered at state level.

* $p < 0.10$ ** $p < 0.05$ *** $p < 0.01$

Table 5.9. Effect of Independent Variables on Turnout and Party over Time

	(1) REPSHARE	(2) REPSHARE	(3) DEMSHARE	(4) DEMSHARE	(5) OTHSHARE	(6) OTHSHARE	(7) TURNOUT	(8) TURNOUT
ID LAW: 2008–2012	0.135 (1.067)		−0.446 (0.972)		0.311* (0.136)		−2.863 (2.143)	
ID LAW: 2012–2016	1.048 (1.112)		0.236 (1.531)		−1.284* (0.585)		−3.911*** (0.766)	
SOFT ID: 2008–2012		1.958*** (0.198)		−1.880*** (0.226)		−0.0775 (0.0389)		−1.925** (0.558)
SOFT ID: 2012–2016		−3.854 (2.446)		4.315 (2.346)		−0.462** (0.140)		−2.481** (0.819)
% Black	−0.626*** (0.0948)	−0.252 (0.300)	0.646*** (0.0947)	0.274 (0.301)	−0.0201*** (0.000897)	−0.0222*** (0.00249)	0.118*** (0.00895)	0.0932 (0.0822)
% Other Race	−0.415*** (0.101)	−1.786** (0.515)	0.436*** (0.0942)	1.694** (0.528)	−0.0218** (0.00796)	0.0928** (0.0277)	−0.108** (0.0422)	0.692** (0.245)
% < 14 years old	0.968** (0.334)	−0.105 (0.182)	−0.917** (0.306)	0.159 (0.180)	−0.0504 (0.0344)	−0.0535*** (0.00630)	0.331 (0.310)	0.327*** (0.0564)
% 15–19 years old	0.975* (0.460)	0.165 (0.360)	−1.073* (0.508)	−0.196 (0.376)	0.0984 (0.0811)	0.0311 (0.0182)	1.652** (0.526)	0.907** (0.238)
% 30–39 years old	0.382 (0.208)	0.907*** (0.190)	−0.445 (0.258)	−0.938*** (0.200)	0.0632 (0.0696)	0.0303* (0.0125)	−0.520 (0.360)	−1.511*** (0.179)

continued on next page

Table 5.9. Continued.

	(1) REPSHARE	(2) REPSHARE	(3) DEMSHARE	(4) DEMSHARE	(5) OTHSHARE	(6) OTHSHARE	(7) TURNOUT	(8) TURNOUT
% 40–59 years old	0.678 (0.356)	1.457*** (0.145)	-0.638 (0.345)	-1.450*** (0.142)	-0.0400 (0.0234)	-0.00634 (0.00906)	1.049*** (0.163)	1.314** (0.293)
% 60 and older	0.933** (0.287)	0.712*** (0.131)	-0.911** (0.277)	-0.690*** (0.130)	-0.0218 (0.0291)	-0.0215*** (0.00174)	0.708*** (0.149)	0.771*** (0.0552)
Unemployment Rate	-1.259*** (0.304)	-2.584* (0.999)	1.204*** (0.307)	2.640* (1.008)	0.0551*** (0.00637)	-0.0561** (0.0127)	0.0115 (0.273)	-0.210 (0.175)
Per Capita Income (1000s)	-0.126 (0.152)	0.135 (0.0829)	0.115 (0.145)	-0.129 (0.0835)	0.0110 (0.00996)	-0.00586 (0.00311)	0.444*** (0.0629)	0.288*** (0.0477)
N	1350	1146	1350	1146	1350	1146	1350	1146
adj. R-sq.	0.817	0.563	0.836	0.570	0.772	0.725	0.457	0.509
Controls	Yes	Yes	Yes	Yes	Yes	Yes	Yes	Yes
Fixed Effects	Yes	Yes	Yes	Yes	Yes	Yes	Yes	Yes

Standard errors in parentheses clustered at state level.

* $p < 0.10$ ** $p < 0.05$ *** $p < 0.01$

Table 5.10. Effect of Independent Variables on Turnout and Party with Interaction Effects

	(1) REPSHARE	(2) REPSHARE	(3) DEMSHARE	(4) DEMSHARE	(5) OTHSHARE	(6) OTHSHARE	(7) TURNOUT	(8) TURNOUT
ID	0.248 (0.667)		0.0980 (0.659)		−0.346 (0.308)		−3.006* (1.389)	
Soft ID		−0.228 (0.878)		0.527 (0.825)		−0.299*** (0.0565)		−1.776** (0.425)
Border	−0.130 (1.427)	5.565** (1.469)	0.131 (1.357)	−5.427** (1.513)	−0.00101 (0.0858)	−0.138 (0.0924)	0.470 (1.032)	0.816 (0.584)
ID x Border	0.787 (0.636)		−0.532 (0.582)		−0.255* (0.108)		−0.914 (1.217)	
Soft ID x Border		−3.961* (1.550)		3.807* (1.523)		0.153 (0.237)		−2.333 (1.120)
% Black	−0.625*** (0.0961)	−0.242 (0.276)	0.646*** (0.0967)	0.264 (0.279)	−0.0215*** (0.00160)	−0.0225*** (0.00306)	0.118*** (0.00803)	0.0964 (0.0848)
% Other Race	−0.413*** (0.103)	−1.741** (0.517)	0.438*** (0.0962)	1.648** (0.532)	−0.0243** (0.00711)	0.0924** (0.0266)	−0.109** (0.0421)	0.684** (0.240)
% < 14 years old	0.957** (0.322)	−0.174 (0.136)	−0.925** (0.299)	0.228 (0.135)	−0.0325 (0.0255)	−0.0537*** (0.00544)	0.346 (0.304)	0.333*** (0.0625)
% 15–19 years old	0.927* (0.416)	0.0569 (0.349)	−1.104** (0.437)	−0.0841 (0.365)	0.177*** (0.0410)	0.0272 (0.0192)	1.702** (0.472)	0.874** (0.238)
% 30–39 years old	0.331* (0.167)	0.772*** (0.0923)	−0.477* (0.202)	−0.798*** (0.0980)	0.146* (0.0698)	0.0268 (0.0140)	−0.480 (0.388)	−1.531*** (0.171)

continued on next page

Table 5.10. Continued.

	(1) REPSHARE	(2) REPSHARE	(3) DEMSHARE	(4) DEMSHARE	(5) OTHSHARE	(6) OTHSHARE	(7) TURNOUT	(8) TURNOUT
% 40–59 years old	0.681 (0.355)	1.390*** (0.134)	-0.631 (0.357)	-1.384*** (0.132)	-0.0498* (0.0252)	-0.00569 (0.00823)	1.045*** (0.168)	1.306** (0.300)
% 60 and older	0.913** (0.263)	0.686** (0.174)	-0.924*** (0.261)	-0.663** (0.175)	0.0107 (0.0146)	-0.0231*** (0.000860)	0.726*** (0.172)	0.766*** (0.0550)
Unemployment Rate	-1.280*** (0.316)	-2.613** (0.932)	1.191*** (0.300)	2.666** (0.948)	0.0884*** (0.0276)	-0.0533** (0.0162)	0.0233 (0.295)	-0.247 (0.168)
Per Capita Income (1000s)	-0.127 (0.149)	0.137 (0.0840)	0.113 (0.145)	-0.131 (0.0846)	0.0138 (0.00910)	-0.00579 (0.00330)	0.445*** (0.0592)	0.286*** (0.0471)
B1 + B3	1.035	-4.189	-0.434	4.334	-0.601	-0.145	-3.921	-4.109
t-Stat	1.526	-1.964	-0.634	2.114	-1.808	-0.571	-3.002	-4.154

Standard errors in parentheses clustered at state level.

* $p < 0.10$ ** $p < 0.05$ *** $p < 0.01$

References

Alrarez, R., Bailey, D. & Katz, J. (2011). An empirical Bayes approach to estimating treatment effects. *Political Analysis, 20*, 20–31.

Ansolabehere, S., Luks, S., & Schaffner, B. (2015). The perils of cherry picking low frequency events in large sample surveys. *Electoral Studies, 40*, 409–10.

Arizona v. Inter Tribal Council of Arizona, Inc. 570 U.S. 1 (2013).

Blake, A. (2016). Republicans keep admitting that voter ID helps them win, for some reason. *Washington Post*. April 7.

Brennan Center for Justice. (2012). *Election 2012: Voting laws roundup*.

Brennan Center for Justice. Undated. *Major litigation that could impact voting access*.

Crawford v. Marion County Election Board 553 U.S. 181 (2008).

Fish v. Kobach 189 F. Supp. 3d 1107 (D. Kan. 2016).

Greenmeier, L. (2008). Many states elect not to use flawed E-voting technology. *Scientific American*. February 12.

Levitt, J. (2007). The truth about voter fraud. New York University: Brennan Institute of Justice.

Lowry, B., & Woodall, H. (2017). Unsealed documents show Kobach urged Trump to change federal voting law. *Kansas City Star*. October 9.

Mataconis, D. (2014). Troubling decision: Federal judge voids changes in Ohio early voting law. *Christian Science Monitor*. September 8.

Minnite, L. (n.d.). The politics of voter fraud. Project vote.org.

Rosenstone, S., & Wolfinger, R. (1978). The effect of registration laws on voter turnout. *American Political Science Review, 72*, 22–45.

Richman, J., Chattha, G., & Earnest, D. (2014). Do non-citizens vote in U.S. elections? *Electoral Studies, 36*, 149–157.

Smith, M., Rackaway, C., & Anderson, K. (2014). *State voting laws in America: Historical statutes and contemporary interpretations*. Palgrave Pivot.

Underhill, W. (n.d.). Voter identification requirements/voter ID laws. National Conference of State Legislatures.

Chapter 6

Contemporary Effects of Felony Disenfranchisement upon Election Turnout and Partisan Vote Share

Linda M. Trautman and Bekah Selby

Introduction

Universal suffrage is a hallmark of a democratic society. However, in recent elections, restrictive felony laws have had a disparate effect upon the voting rights of many American citizens, disproportionately racial minorities. In the twenty-first century, state felony laws appear to have been an effective strategy in reducing the voting power of minorities—in particular, African Americans (King & Erickson, 2016; King, 2017; Brown-Dean, 2011). However, the results of empirical research are mixed when it comes to measuring the impact of felony disenfranchisement on voter turnout and partisan vote share.

    A long history of minority exclusion from electoral participation and the body politic has been a fundamental problem, undermining representative governance and political fairness within the United States. Many traditional impediments to voting such as the poll tax and literacy tests were eradicated as a result of the Twenty-Fourth Amendment and the Voting Rights Act of 1965. However, legal and structural barriers to the franchise remain a formidable challenge for minority communities.

Critics fear that a consequential and systemic effect of felony laws will be minority vote dilution, impeding political empowerment and representation of minority communities, and even altering election results and turnout (King & Erickson, 2016; Berman, 2015; Pettus, 2013; Manza & Uggen, 2006).

Prior to the 2016 presidential election, intense efforts to suppress the voting rights of people convicted of felonies occurred in major battleground states. New restrictive post-sentencing requirements were instituted in states such as Iowa. The 2016 presidential election, therefore, is ideal for investigating the hypothesis that felony disenfranchisement laws positively increased Republican vote share yet reduced overall levels of voter mobilization and turnout.

The issue is particularly acute given the growth in mass incarceration of African Americans (see Bobo & Thompson, 2010) and the disparity in felony conviction rates among racial minorities. In 2007, African American males constituted 39 percent while Latinos comprised about 20 percent of the prison population (Bobo & Thompson, 2010). While social scientists and legal scholars recognize the significance of race in the enactment of state felony laws (Allen, 2011; Fletcher, 1999; Hull, 2006; Uggen & Manza, 2002, 2004, 2006; Preuh, 2001) research on their impact is limited within the extant literature. Does felony disenfranchisement, in general, negatively affect election outcomes? More specifically, does the disenfranchisement of felons/ex-felons reduce overall voter turnout and participation rates of minorities?

A few legal scholars maintain that the affected population is less likely to vote even when states enact liberal reforms to extend the franchise. Contrary to this view, empirical research suggests that reenfranchisement of ex-felons/felons is critical to preventing minority vote dilution (Behrens et al., 2003; Uggen et al., 2003) and may reverse political outcomes (Manza & Uggen, 2004). It reduces the participatory effects of the carceral state (Gerber et al., 2015). Another perspective is offered by Katherine Pettus (2013), who notes that felony disenfranchisement compromises the citizenship regime as espoused by the equal protection clause of the Fourteenth Amendment, especially for the African American community. Felony laws significantly restrict electoral participation and voting power of African Americans, even those who are still able to vote. Pettus argues that criminal disenfranchisement undermines the ideals of American democracy.

Origins of Felon Disenfranchisement

Prior to 1840, a small number of states enacted felony disenfranchisement statutes. During the first wave of felony disenfranchisement, approximately four out of 26 states adopted felony statues. An increase in the rate of state adoption of felony laws took place between 1840 and 1861. A total of fourteen states established felony disenfranchisement laws. However, during the Civil War and the Reconstruction period, massive resistance to the voting rights of felons occurred as states passed more restrictive laws (Uggen et al., 2003). According to Liles (2007), by the time of the Civil War, felony laws had been established in twenty states. By 1869, nine additional states enacted felon disenfranchisement provisions (Liles, 2007). Scholars have noted the origins of the racial intent of felony laws date back to the Civil War Era (Fellner & Mauer, 1998; Uggen et al., 2003; Manza & Uggen, 2004). Immediately after the Civil War, there was significant progress in advancing the suffrage and citizenship rights of racial minorities. The Fourteenth Amendment upheld equal citizenship rights while the Fifteenth Amendment granted the franchise to Black men. Unfortunately, many states responded with laws designed to mitigate this progress. It was during this period of backlash that restrictive felon disenfranchisement laws were established. The rigid implementation of felony laws was most prevalent in Southern states. Manza and Uggen (2004) and Uggen et al. (2003) found that between 1850 and 2002, states with higher proportions of nonwhites were significantly more likely to enact punitive felony disenfranchisement legislation. Further, Preuhs (2001) argued that a strong relationship exists between the size of the minority population (Black or Latino) in a state and the severity of felon laws.

During the twentieth century, most notably between the 1950s and 1970s, the pattern of felony disenfranchisement changed as a result of liberal reforms. The effect was a decline in the number of states disenfranchising ex-felons (Manza & Uggen, 2006). Liberalization of felony laws was likely a result of high levels of social and civil rights activism during the 1960s and 1970s (Manza & Uggen, 2004). Increasing insurgency among racial minorities might have resulted in greater policy responsiveness to race-based policies from state elites, who in turn acted to soften or repeal felony disenfranchisement laws in some—but not all—states during this period.

Contemporary Felony Disenfranchisement and Battleground States in the 2016 Presidential Election

Today, massive efforts have been instituted to undermine the gains of the voting rights movement. According to Michelle Alexander (2012), mass incarceration of African American men constitutes a deleterious effort to undermine the gains of the civil rights movement. She argues that mass incarceration of African American men represents the "New Jim Crow" era. In 1970 during the pre–war on drugs era, the total state and federal prisoner population constituted 48,497. The Black prison population was comprised of 19,143 individuals and the White prison population consisted of 29,154 (Langan, 1991). In 2017, the total state and federal Black prisoner population was 475,900 while the overall Latino prisoner population consisted of 336,500 incarcerees (Bronson & Carson, 2019; The Sentencing Project, 2019).

Alexander (2012) asserts that implementation of restrictive felony disenfranchisement laws is a further manifestation of such initiatives. Statewide campaigns to repress voting rights of felons and ex-felons were aggressively pursued in the wake of the 2016 presidential election in major battleground states. Florida, Iowa, and Virginia developed post-sentencing felony requirements. Although policy reforms of felony laws were enacted through executive actions in key swing states in 2011, major efforts to push more stringent laws emerged closer to the 2016 presidential election. Legislation was put into force to promote permanent felony disenfranchisement. The percentage of the voting-age population disenfranchised in these states ranged from none (Maine, Vermont) to 3 percent of the voting-age population (Georgia) in the 2016 presidential election (United States Election Project, 2016)

Contemporary Regional and State Variations in Felony Statues

Varied patterns of state restrictions exist today. A few of the Northeastern states have the most liberal felony laws (Allen, 2010). In addition, in light of the 2000 presidential election and legal challenges about the constitutionality of felon disenfranchisement, some states including Connecticut, New Mexico, Nevada, and Maryland reformed their voting laws. Historically, many Southern states (e.g., Kentucky and Virginia) retained the most restrictive felon rules. However, state executive action and constitutional measures have been put forth to mitigate harsh felony laws. In 2016, for example, Virginia governor Terry McAuliffe manually signed restoration voting rights for about 13,000 felons with the goal of reinstating 200,000 felons' voter rights by April 2016 (Newkirk, 2018). A major statewide campaign to restore felony voting rights also took place in Florida in 2018. The ballot initiative, which struck down restrictive felony laws in Florida, passed by an overwhelming majority during the 2018 midterm elections. In November 2018, Florida voters decided on a constitutional amendment to restore felony voting rights (Levy, 2018). Amendment 4 was also a ban on the post-sentencing felony disenfranchisement provisions instituted in Florida.

Maine and Vermont are the only two states that permit the lifelong enfranchisement of felons/ex-felons. In contrast, Virginia and Kentucky historically required a lifelong voting ban for felons/ex-felons. More recently, these states have established reform policies that have relaxed felony voting rights prohibitions. The regions of the country that tend to have the most repressive forms of felony laws are the Deep South (for example, Georgia, Mississippi, and Alabama) and a few Western states. The racial disparity in felony laws has far-reaching effects in these regions. The analysis below reflects the racial and regional effects of felony disenfranchisement for African Americans. More recent efforts have been waged to further suppress voting protections of felons and ex-felons. Most notably, post-sentencing requirements that stripped voting privileges from felons.

Assessing the Effects of Felony Disenfranchisement upon Voter Turnout

Scholarly research on felony disenfranchisement has assessed the impact of these laws upon voter turnout in American elections. The extant literature suggests that contemporary rates of felony disenfranchisement affect electoral outcomes (Uggen & Manza, 2002; Manza & Uggen, 2004, 2006; Miles, 2004). In a longitudinal analysis, Uggen & Manza (2006), for example, argue that the election turnout rates in the 2000 presidential election, along with certain U.S. Senate races in the 1970s and 1980s, would have changed substantively if felons had been granted the right to vote. They reported that in highly contested elections, voter participation of felons would have altered the electoral margins in favor of Democrats in the 2000 presidential election and in Senate elections since 1986. The analysis indicates that 27.2 percent of felons (if granted the right to vote) would have voted (Manza & Uggen, 2004). In a subsequent study, Manza and Uggen implicitly argue that disallowing ex-felons the right to vote compromised electoral outcomes in three U.S. Senate elections in 1978 (Virginia), 1984, and 1998 (Kentucky).

Other research focuses more specifically on the laws' impact among African Americans. A study by McLeod, White, and Gavin (2003) indicated that felony disenfranchisement significantly and negatively affects state-level voter turnout for the otherwise eligible, voting-age African American population, especially those who reside in states with restrictive felony disenfranchisement statues. Bowers and Preuhs's (2009) study further confirms the disparate effects of felony disenfranchisement upon African Americans relative to other demographic groups.

Drawing upon a case study analysis of North Carolina, Jackson-Gleich (2006) examined the systemic impact of felony laws upon voter turnout of felons and nonfelons. Contrary to previous studies, she finds that the percentage of disenfranchised felons does not impact voter participation levels of eligible voters. Essentially, although she notes the harmful effects of felony laws upon the voting rights of felons and ex-felons, her findings ultimately suggest that the impact will be lessened, since felony disenfranchisement appears to have negligible consequences for voter turnout rates of eligible African American voters. An underlying limitation of the study is the ability to evaluate broadly the influence of felony laws upon election outcomes given the single-state analysis.

Some research adopts more sophisticated, quantitative methods. For example, Thomas Miles (2004) used an econometric model to estimate the effects of felony disenfranchisement upon state-level voter turnout. His analysis suggested that felon disfranchisement has no effect upon voter turnout, most notably the voting rates of African American males.

Social science research has advanced our understanding of the effects of felon disenfranchisement upon American voter turnout and political outcomes in general; however, a paucity of research exists regarding the estimated aggregate impact of felon disenfranchisement laws upon voter participation and turnout in more recent elections, such as the 2016 presidential election. The present study seeks to address this shortcoming.

Contemporary Effects and Racial Impact of State Felony Laws on African Americans

Current data indicate that approximately 6.1 million Americans are impacted by felony disenfranchisement (The Sentencing Project, 2018;

Chung, 2019; Uggen, Larson, & Shannon, 2016). While the overall trend in the rate of felon disenfranchisement continues to grow among the U.S. population, the statistics show that the political impact of felony laws on African Americans is substantial and continues to rise. Recent estimates reflect that more than two million African Americans are disenfranchised because of felony convictions. Of that number, roughly one million are ex-felons who have completed their sentences (The Sentencing Project, 2018).

Overall, approximately 7.7 percent of the African American population is barred from voting because of felony laws, while only about 1.8 percent of the non–African American population is affected by felony disenfranchisement (Uggen et al., 2016). Thus, relative to other racial groups, African Americans are disproportionately overrepresented in terms of felony disenfranchisement.

Recent estimates indicate great variation in the Black disenfranchisement rate. The range of the percentage of Black citizens affected by felony disenfranchisement in the Northeast was 0.0–1.36. In that region, New Jersey was the state with the highest proportion of disenfranchised felons as of 2016. In sharp contrast, the lowest felon disenfranchisement rates are found in Maine and Vermont, because these states do not restrict the right to vote for felons/ex-felons. In the Midwest, the percentage of Black disenfranchised varied from 2.0–9.8, with Iowa ranking as the highest in terms of proportion of Black felon disenfranchisement, while Illinois comprised the lowest.

The gross disparity in the range of felony disenfranchisement is most apparent in the South. Florida and Virginia contained among the highest aggregate percentage of Black felons in 2016. Virginia, most notably, has enacted very restrictive felony laws, which prohibit lifelong denial of the franchise to felons and ex-felons. Prior to the recent reforms of felony laws passed by voters in Florida, estimates indicated that Black felons constituted 21.4 percent of the disenfranchised population. Relative to

Table 6.1. Aggregate and Black Disenfranchisement (Percentage of the VAP) by Region, 2016

Region	Aggregate Disenfranchisement	Black Disenfranchisement
Northeast	0.0–1.36	0.0–5.3
Midwest	0.4–2.2	2.0–9.8
South	0.5–10.4	1.1–21.9
West	0.4–5.3	1.02–18.29

the total percent disenfranchised in every state, the proportion of Black disenfranchisement exceeded the total percent disenfranchised. Despite some recent state-led reform efforts, higher levels of Black disenfranchisement are still prevalent in certain states.

Formal Hypotheses

The first hypothesis is that aggregate felony disenfranchisement depresses state-level voter turnout. Exclusionary policies that deprive significant proportions of citizens from exercising the franchise will likely have systemic negative effects upon election outcomes and voter turnout regardless of demographic factors. Thus, as the percentage of felony disenfranchisement increases in a state, voter turnout decreases in a state.

Further, given grave inequities in the criminal justice system, high incarceration rates of African American males, and disproportionate numbers of African Americans convicted of felonies, a second hypothesis predicts that aggregate Black felony disenfranchisement negatively affects voter turnout and participation. As the percentage of Black felony disenfranchisement increases, presumably Black voter turnout decreases. The theoretical underpinning of the hypothesis is that the proportion of the Black enfranchised population will be negatively impacted in terms of voter turnout due to the large proportion of Black felony disenfranchisement at the state level of analysis. An underlying assumption of the research is that felon disenfranchisement undermines the political power of minority communities.

Data and Methods

The data for the current analysis derive from varied sources. Aggregate state-level data on the proportion of felony disenfranchisement and African American felony disenfranchisement for the 2016 presidential election derive from the Sentencing Project (www.sentencingproject.org). Felony disenfranchisement, an independent variable, is measured as the disenfranchised population as a percent of the voting-age population (VAP) by state (Uggen, Larson, & Shannon, 2016). The analysis is based upon the 2016 presidential election because many states aggressively instituted new restrictive felony requirements.

Estimates on county-level voter turnout were obtained from the U.S. Census Bureau Current Population Survey Voting and Registration Supplement. The Current Population Survey (CPS) is conducted by the U.S. Census Bureau and consists of a monthly survey with approximately 50,000 households. A series of questions are asked about voting behavior, demographic, and socioeconomic factors. Two dependent variables are employed to understand the political consequences of felony disenfranchisement upon election turnout. Additional data to estimate the level of turnout by state are obtained through the United States Election Project. The first dependent variable, overall voter turnout, is measured as the percentage of the VEP that turn out to vote. The second dependent variable, Republican vote share is measured as the change in the proportion of Republican votes.

Voter Turnout of African Americans in the 2016 Presidential Election

According to the U.S. Census Current Population Survey (CPS) data (2016), American voter turnout in the 2016 presidential election was approximately 61 percent. African American voter turnout was about 55.9 percent in the 2016 presidential election, which reflects a noticeable decline from the 2012 presidential election. Black turnout in the 2012 presidential election was approximately 66.6 percent (Current Population Survey, 2017).

Changing voting patterns of minority groups, notably African Americans, in the 2016 presidential election reflect the importance of addressing structural factors, such as felony laws. Lower voter participation and turnout among African Americans raises the query of whether or not the rate of Black felony disenfranchisement suppressed voting in the 2016 presidential election.

Preliminary Findings and Results

State fixed effects regression analyses were utilized to measure the impact of felony disenfranchisement upon the change in Republican party vote share and percentage change in voter turnout from 2012–16. The analysis examined both the aggregate (county-level) and individual-level effect.

Table 6.2. State Fixed Regression of the Effects of Felony Disenfranchisement upon Turnout

	(1) Δ % GOP (2012–2016)	(2) Δ % Turnout (2012–2016)	(3) Δ % GOP (2012–2016)	(4) Δ % Turnout (2012–2016)
Aggregate Felony Disenfranchisement	3.243*** (0.915)	−11.61*** (0.418)		
Black Felony Disenfranchisement			0.312*** (0.0879)	−1.117*** (0.0402)
Δ % 3rd Party (2012–2016)	−0.825*** (0.140)		−0.825*** (0.140)	
Δ % Turnout (2012–2016)	−0.0117 (0.0244)		−0.0117 (0.0244)	
% < 20	−0.218*** (0.0653)	−0.234*** (0.0731)	−0.218*** (0.0653)	−0.234*** (0.0731)
% > 65	−0.0451 (0.0462)	−0.0531 (0.0356)	−0.0451 (0.0462)	−0.0531 (0.0356)
% Female	0.0442 (0.0566)	0.0944** (0.0512)	0.0442 (0.0566)	0.0944** (0.0512)
% Black	−0.0717*** (0.0147)	−0.104*** (0.00830)	−0.0717*** (0.0147)	−0.104*** (0.00830)

% Other Race	0.0170	−0.0187**	0.0170	−0.0187**
	(0.0185)	(0.0111)	(0.0185)	(0.0111)
% Less than HS Diploma	−0.167***	0.0240	−0.167***	0.0240
	(0.0278)	(0.0256)	(0.0278)	(0.0256)
% Bachelors or Higher	−0.358***	−0.0548*	−0.358***	−0.0548*
	(0.0237)	(0.0211)	(0.0237)	(0.0211)
Per Capita Income ($1000s)	−0.0129	−0.0175	−0.0129	−0.0175
	(0.0114)	(0.0198)	(0.0114)	(0.0198)
% Poverty	0.0632*	−0.0376**	0.0632**	−0.0376**
	(0.0375)	(0.0207)	(0.0375)	(0.0207)
% Unemployed	0.140	0.0735	0.140	0.0735
	(0.0912)	(0.0550)	(0.0912)	(0.0550)
Competitiveness	24.19***	−76.90***	6.370***	−13.10***
	(5.939)	(2.727)	(0.968)	(0.474)
N	3034	3034	3034	3034
adj. R-squared	0.811	0.440	0.811	0.440

Standard errors clustered at state level in parenthesis.

* $p < 0.05$ ** $p < 0.10$ *** $p < 0.01$

Models 1 and 2 present the results of the impact of felony disenfranchisement on county-level vote share and turnout (see Table 6.2). These findings suggest that an increase in county felony disenfranchisement is associated with an increase in the share of Republican votes even controlling for many other determinants of this variable. Additionally, the results indicate that a unit increase in county felony disenfranchisement is associated with a decrease of voter turnout of 11.61 percent between the 2012 to 2016 presidential elections. Partisan gaps in vote share and turnout between the Democratic and Republican parties are linked to the disparate impact of felony laws upon the poor and African Americans. Generally, such populations tend to ally with the Democratic Party coalition. Evidence presented here indicates that Republicans are electorally advantaged by felony disenfranchisement, relative to Democrats.

The analyses also show the effects of Black disenfranchisement upon party vote share and election turnout in Models 3 and 4 (see Table 6.2). The predictions are consistent with the aggregate disenfranchisement models. A unit increase in Black disenfranchisement resulted in an increase of 0.312 percent of Republican share of the vote. Effects of felony disenfranchisement are more evidently impactful upon African Americans and communities of color, which poses negative consequences for their overall voting power. The existence of felony disenfranchisement, therefore, dilutes the vote share for the Democratic Party and advantages the Republican Party since African Americans constitute a core base of support for the Democratic Party. Further, the results provide evidence that as level of Black disenfranchisement increases, there is a statistically significant decline in voter turnout rates. Higher rates of aggregate Black disenfranchisement significantly undercut the potential overall electoral clout of African Americans.

In all of the empirical models, we include a series of standard demographic and socioeconomic variables predictive of voter behavior. These are control variables, and the coefficients of these variables are consistent with theory and previous literature. Additionally, we included a measure of state electoral competitiveness to capture the impact of a county within a state considered as a "swing" state during the 2016 presidential election. The results indicate that counties in states with high levels of electoral competitiveness had higher levels of Republican vote shares. However, we find that counties in electorally competitive states had lower voter turnouts in 2016 compared to 2012. Such result warrants further empirical exploration.

Overall, the results indicate that felony disenfranchisement has a statistically significant impact on voter behavior. Our estimates suggest that restrictive voter laws may favor conservative political parties and reduce voter turnout. This result is particularly salient when considering only Black voter disenfranchisement.

Conclusion

Felony disenfranchisement presents a contemporary challenge to democratic fairness and equality. As a result of current strategies to suppress voting rights, attention to the potential deleterious effects of felony laws is very important. Wide disparities within the criminal justice system and the application of felony laws represent the need for systemic reform in order to ensure that the right to vote is protected for all groups. Critical contentions of this research are that felony laws might have a broad effect in reducing the voting strength and rates of various demographic groups, most notably African Americans. Implications of this research relate to the Supreme Court case *Shelby County v Holder* (2013) which challenged key provisions of the Voting Rights Act of 1965, Section 4, based upon the formula coverage, and Section 5, based upon the pre-clearance requirement. Essentially, the Court ruled that these provisions were no longer needed because voting parity has been achieved between races. The disproportionate criminalization of African Americans and the systemic impact of felony laws on minority communities, in particular, jeopardizes voting and representational parity of African Americans.

Effects of contemporary felon disenfranchisement upon election outcomes likely vary according to region, the political culture, and the severity of the felon disenfranchisement statutes in each state. African Americans are exponentially affected by felon disenfranchisement in Deep South states, given the large concentration of the Black population and the magnitude of felony disenfranchisement in the South. I assess that ascriptive hierarchy, a concept referring to inegalitarian social relations and racial inequality in American politics, as described by political scientist Rogers M. Smith (1993), has been a defining feature of deep Southern states. The severity of felony laws, therefore, is extremely problematic. Regardless of region, minority felon disenfranchisement compromises civic equality and political representation. Consistent with Preuhs's (2001) view, the existence of voting bans on felons/ex-felons compromises the procedural aspect of democracy. Existence of felony disenfranchisement also calls into question the substantive dimension of democracy that involves a commitment to inclusiveness and equality. Recent reform initiatives, such as Amendment 4 in Florida, which overwhelmingly passed in support of restoring voting rights for felons, are necessary to protect democracy for all Americans. Although the Florida measure has experienced significant challenges from the Republican governor Ron DeSantis and the Florida State Supreme Court, the protections of felony voting rights have been upheld in Florida. In June 2020, a U.S. District Court struck down a 2019 Republican pay-to-vote law that required the payment of all fees, fines and restitution in order for felons to vote (The Sentencing Project, 2020). In addition to Florida and Iowa, Kentucky was among the three states that permanently disenfranchised felons. In 2019, however, Kentucky Democratic governor Andy Beshear issued an executive order to restore voting rights to about 140,000 felons (The Sentencing Project, 2020). The current research suggests that further policy reforms and movements to reverse state felony laws are critical for full inclusion of all Americans, notably African Americans and the poor, in a functioning and healthy democratic polity.

References

Alexander, M. (2012). The new Jim Crow: Mass incarceration in an age of colorblindness. The New Press.

Allen, J. (2011). Documentary disenfranchisement. *Tulane Law Review*, 86, 389–605.

Bronson, J., & Carson, E. A. (2019). Prisoners in 2017. Bureau of Justice Statistics.

Brown-Dean, K. (2011). Permanent outsiders: Felon disenfranchisement and the breakdown of Black politics. *National Political Science Review*.

Bobo, L., & Thompson, V. (2010). Racialized mass incarceration: Poverty, prejudice, and punishment. In H. R. Markus & P. M. L. Moya (Eds.), *Doing race: 21 essays for the 21st century*. W. W. Norton.

Bowers, M., & Preuhs, R. (2009). Collateral consequences of a collateral penalty: The negative effect of felon disenfranchisement laws on the political participation of nonfelons. *Social Science Quarterly*, 90(3), 722–743.

Chung, J. (2019). *A felony disenfranchisement: A primer*. The Sentencing Project.

Fellner, J., & Mauer, M. (1998). *Losing the vote: The impact of felony disenfranchisement laws in the United States*. Human Rights Watch and the Sentencing Project.

Fletcher, G. (1999). Disenfranchisement as punishment: Reflections on the racial uses of *Infamia*. *UCLA Law Review*, 46, 1895–1908.
Hull, E. (2006). *The disenfranchisement of ex-felons*. Temple University Press.
Jackson-Gleich, G. (2006). The broad impact of felony disenfranchisement: How political exclusion affects felons, non-felons, and the nation. Manuscript.
King, B., & Erickson, L. (2016). Disenfranchising the enfranchised: Exploring the relationship between felony disenfranchisement and African American voter turnout. *Journal of Black Studies*, 47(8), 1–23.
King, R. (2009). Challenging disenfranchisement for felony convictions. *Human Rights*, 36(2), 18.
King, R. (2017). Challenging disenfranchisement for felony convictions. Human Rights Magazine, http: www.americanbar.org.
Langan, P. (1991). Race of prisoners admitted to state and federal institutions, 1926–1986. U.S. Department of Justice, Office of Justice Programs, and Bureau of Justice Statistics.
Levy, P. (2018). Judge strikes down felon disenfranchisement system in Florida. www.motherjones.com.
Liles, W. (2007). Challenges to disenfranchisement laws: Past, present, and future. *Alabama Law Review*, 58(3), 615–629.
Manza, J., & Uggen, C. (2004). Punishment and democracy: Disenfranchisement of nonincarcerated felons in the United States. *Perspectives on Politics*, 2(3), 491–505.
Manza, J., & Uggen, C. (2006). *Locked out: Felon disenfranchisement and American democracy*. Oxford University Press.
Maldef, Uggen, C., & Manza, J. (2003). Diminished voting power in the Latino community: The impact of felony disenfranchisement in ten selected States. Manuscript.
McLeod, A., White, I., & Gavin, A. (2003). The locked ballot box: The impact of state criminal disenfranchisement laws on African American voting behavior and implications for reform. *Virginia Journal of Social Policy and the Law*.
Miles, T. (2004). Felon disenfranchisement and voter turnout. *The Journal of Legal Studies*, 33, 85–129.
Newkirk, Vann II. (2018). How letting felons vote is changing Virginia. *The Atlantic*.
Pettus, K. (2013). Felony disenfranchisement in America: Historical origins, institutional racism, and modern consequences. State University of New York Press.
Preuhs, R. (2001). State felon disenfranchisement policy. *Social Science Quarterly*, 82, 733748.
Shelby County v. Holder 570 US 529 (2013).
Smith, R. (1993). Beyond Tocqueville, Myrdal, and Hartz: The multiple traditions in America. *American Political Science Review*, 87(3), 549–566.

The Sentencing Project. (2018). Expanding the vote: Two decades of felony disenfranchisement

The Sentencing Project. (2019). Trends in U.S. corrections: U.S. state and prisoner population, 1925–2017.

The Sentencing Project. (2020). Disenfranchisement news: Judge strikes down Florida's pay-to-vote system.

Uggen, C., & Manza, J. (2002). Democratic contraction? Political consequences of felon disenfranchisement in the United States. *American Sociological Review, 67,* 777–803.

Uggen, C., Manza, J., & Behrens, A. (2003). Felony voting rights and the disenfranchisement of African Americans. *Souls, 5*(3), 48–57.

Uggen, C., Shannon, S., & Manza, J. 2016. State-level estimates of felony disenfranchisement in the United States (2016). In Uggen, C., Larson, R., & Shannon, S., *Six million lost Voters: State-level estimates of felony disenfranchisement in the United States.*

U.S. Census Bureau. (2017). Current population survey.

Wolfinger, R., & Rosenstone, S. (1980). *Who votes?* Yale University Press.

Chapter 7

Using Mathematics to Understand How Gerrymandering Affects Partisan Voting Power

Brian Hollenbeck and Deborah G. Hann

Introduction

While some laws are brazen in their attempt to disadvantage voters, other methods can be more subtle. For example, the changing of district boundaries can dramatically influence elections, even though individual voters may be unaware that the impact of their vote has been changed. However, it is not always clear how to draw district boundaries to achieve a fair outcome. Mathematics can help us understand how to identify and analyze potential partisan gerrymandering.

In its recent *Rucho v Common Cause* ruling, the U.S. Supreme Court greatly limited the role of the courts in limiting partisan gerrymandering. Upholding the *Davis v Bandemer* case of 1976, the court reaffirmed that partisan gerrymandering is a "political question" and refused to intervene. In *Rucho*, the Court found that "None of the proposed 'tests' for evaluating partisan gerrymandering claims meets the need for a limited and precise standard that is judicially discernible and manageable." They also noted that racial gerrymandering may be held to a different standard, because "race-based decisionmaking . . . is 'inherently suspect' [as per] *Miller v. Johnson* [1995]."

The struggle to identify and analyze instances of potential partisan gerrymandering is more than 200 years old. The crux of this struggle can be reduced to one main question: Was a state's congressional district map intentionally drawn to manipulate the outcome to favor one political party? There are four main criteria one can check to determine if a district map should be flagged for potential partisan gerrymandering:

1. Does a district contain significantly more or fewer voters than another?
2. Does the shape of a district appear to be unnatural and thus indicate manipulation?
3. Does the distribution of voters among the districts negatively affect one party more than another in an election?
4. Does the outcome of a potential election for a particular district map drastically differ from the expected outcome of a nonpartisan map?

In recent years, mathematics has been playing an important role in quantifying these criteria in an objective and meaningful way. We will analyze these four criteria in more detail from this mathematical perspective.

Example

Let us consider a simple example to help us understand current mathematical approaches to analyzing potential gerrymandered districts. Suppose a state (call it Lyon) of 100 voters are to be split among four districts. Each voter belongs to party X or party O. Assume 52 percent of Lyon votes for party X. For now, let us assume the votes are distributed randomly within Lyon. Figure 7.1 shows such a possible configuration.

O	O	X	O	O	X	O	O	O	X
X	X	X	O	X	O	X	O	O	X
X	X	O	O	X	O	O	O	O	O
O	O	X	O	O	X	O	X	X	X
X	X	O	O	X	O	X	X	O	X
O	X	O	X	O	O	X	X	O	X
X	O	X	X	X	O	O	X	O	O
O	X	X	O	O	X	X	X	X	X
X	O	O	O	O	O	X	O	X	X
X	X	X	X	X	X	O	X	O

Figure 7.1. Hypothetical Distribution of 100 Voters in "Lyon."

We wish to draw four districts to divide these 100 voters. Consider the first criterion mentioned in the introduction. This criterion is known as "one-person, one-vote" and is simple to check.[1] It argues that "votes of people in overpopulated districts held less value than those of people in less-populated districts, and that this inequality violated the Equal Protection Clause of the Fourteenth Amendment," a claim made by the plaintiffs in *Rucho* (2019, p. 11). This criterion requires that each district contain approximately the same number of voters. If we assume each district of Lyon should contain an equal number of voters, there are 1.6×10^{57} possible configurations to create four such districts. This is approximately equivalent to the number of hydrogen atoms in our sun. To consider just a few cases among this myriad of possibilities, Figures 7.2, 7.3, and 7.4 show three possible district maps for Lyon:

O	O	X	O	O	X	O	O	O	X
X	X	X	O	X	O	X	O	O	X
X	X	O	O	X	O	O	O	O	O
O	O	X	O	O	X	O	X	X	X
X	X	O	O	X	O	X	X	O	X
O	X	O	X	O	O	X	X	O	X
X	O	X	X	X	O	O	X	O	O
O	X	X	O	O	X	X	X	X	X
X	O	O	O	O	O	X	O	X	X
X	X	X	X	X	X	X	O	X	O

Figure 7.2. First Hypothetical Four-District Map for "Lyon."

---

1. Let A, B ⊆ $[0.1]^2$ be disjoint finite sets that correspond to voter locations from two parties. Assume k districts, $D_1, \ldots, D_k$, partition the set, $[0,1]^2$. To enforce the One-person, One-vote criteria, notice there exists $\delta \in [0,1]$ such that the districts always satisfy

$$(1-\delta)[\frac{|A \cup B|}{k}] \leq |(A \cup B) \cap D_i| \leq (1+\delta)[\frac{|A \cup B|}{k}] \; \forall i \in \{1, \ldots, k\}.$$

The middle term quantifies the number of voters in each district. Choosing δ near 0 assures each district will be within a small tolerance of the average number of voters in each district (Alexeev & Mixon, 2018).

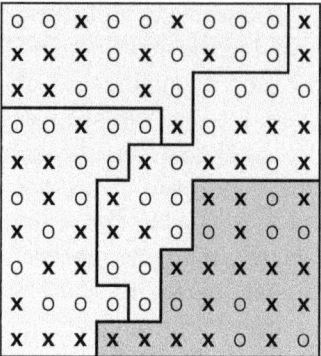

Figure 7.3. Second Hypothetical Four-District Map for "Lyon."

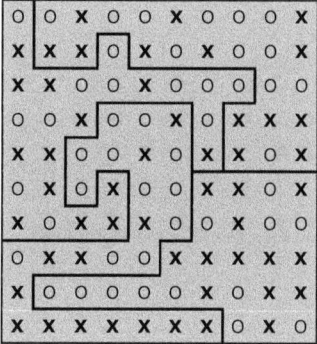

Figure 7.4. Third Hypothetical Four-District Map for "Lyon."

To the casual observer, the shapes of the districts in Figure 7.2 look more natural than the other two figures. In addition, the outcome of each party winning two seats matches our expectation for a state where one party has a slim 52–48 advantage. Figures 7.3 and 7.4 illustrate maps that are suspicious in both shape and results. We need an objective way to quantify this observation. Criterion #2 applies when analyzing the shape of a district.

The second criterion stems from the original case of gerrymandering, where the bizarre shape of a state senate election district in Massachusetts provoked a political cartoon mocking its likeness to a salamander (Alexeev & Mixon, 2018). States have tried to combat this by requiring the shapes of districts to be "compact." Intuitively, this means the border of each district should not zigzag unnecessarily around the state. Mathematically, a square is the most compact shape possible for Lyon.[2] But extra constraints such as county lines, rivers, mountains, and population centers necessitate the need for exceptions. Thus, deviation from perfection is to be expected for most districts in most states. To quantify the magnitude of this deviation, mathematicians have created several definitions for compactness (Azavea, 2019).

Let us examine four of the most common definitions. For each example, we scale the definition so that a square has a compactness score of exactly 1. Less-compact shapes have scores closer to 0. One perimeter-based definition is known as Polsby-Popper, introduced in 1991 (Alexeev & Mixon, 2018). The Polsby-Popper score uses the ratio of the district's area to the square of its perimeter.[3] This method is advantageous because it is simple to understand and penalizes any shape that meanders a lot. However, this means that any district with long borders due to rivers or other physical obstacles will also be penalized. For our example, all four districts must contain the same area. Thus, as a district's perimeter increases, its compactness score will decrease. See Tables 7.1 and 7.2 for the score for each district in Figures 7.3 and 7.4. Notice this score identifies District 2 as the least compact of Figure 7.3 and District 3 as the least compact of Figure 7.4. These scores show the districts of Figure 4 are, on average, less compact than the districts of Figure 7.3. This corresponds to our intuition of what it means to be "compact."

A second definition makes use of the convex hull of a district. The *convex hull* can be thought of as the shape a rubber band would make if it were wrapped around the boundary of the district.[4] The score

---

2. A circle is considered the only perfectly compact shape since it uses the least perimeter to enclose a given area. Since curved boundaries are not practical for our example, we will tweak standard compactness definitions so that a square is the most ideal shape possible.

3. The Polsby-Popper compactness score for a district, D, is given by $PP(D) := \frac{4\pi |D|}{|\delta D|^2}$ where $|\delta D|$ denotes the perimeter of the district and $|D|$ denotes its area. Notice for any possible district, $0 < PP(D) \leq 1$, with equality at 1 being achieved when D is a circle (Alexeev & Mixon, 2018). We will adjust the definition slightly so that a square scores as maximally compact: $\widetilde{PP}(D) := \frac{16|D|}{|\delta D|^2}$.

4. More precisely, the convex hull is the minimum convex polygon that can enclose a district (Azavea, 2019). A polygon is convex if all of its interior angles are less than 180 degrees.

is calculated by finding the ratio of the district's area and the area of its convex hull. This score can sometimes be easier to calculate than a perimeter-based score since the hull "smooths" convoluted edges. However, this feature might minimize the impact of gerrymandering on a district's score. Notice that the convex hull scores are generally more than the perimeter scores, indicating that meandering districts are penalized less with the convex hull score than with the perimeter-based score. Nevertheless, both scores agree that the districts of Figure 7.4 are less compact than those of Figure 7.3.

The last two definitions of compactness to consider also compare the ratio of the district's area and the area of an enclosing polygon. In one case, this polygon is the smallest square that can enclose the district; in another, the smallest rectangle.[5] These are both simple to calculate and understand. However, scores can be misleading since a district with a large distance in one dimension will automatically have a low compactness score, regardless of how much the boundary meanders. For example, notice that Districts 1 and 2 have the same square compactness score, even though the perimeter score is much higher for District 1. Using a minimizing bounding rectangle improves this inconsistency, as shown in Tables 7.1 and 7.2. As expected, rectangle compactness scores will be higher than the corresponding square scores.

Table 7.1. Compactness Scores for "Lyon" Map in Figure 7.3

	District 1	District 2	District 3	District 4	Average
Perimeter	0.592	**0.391**	0.592	0.694	0.567
Convex Hull	0.820	**0.641**	0.806	0.862	0.782
Square	**0.309**	**0.309**	0.510	0.510	0.410
Rectangle	0.694	**0.463**	0.714	0.714	0.646

Table 7.2. Compactness Scores for "Lyon" Map in Figure 7.4

	District 1	District 2	District 3	District 4	Average
Perimeter	0.227	0.391	**0.207**	0.510	0.334
Convex Hull	**0.581**	0.694	0.617	0.725	0.654
Square	0.391	**0.309**	0.510	**0.309**	0.380
Rectangle	**0.446**	0.556	0.510	0.556	0.517

---

5. This is known as the Reock metric if we instead enclose with the minimum bounding circle (Azavea, 2019).

Overall, the compactness scores generally match perception with lower scores corresponding to the districts with shapes that appear to be manipulated to achieve a particular outcome. It is interesting to note that each compactness score identifies a different district in Figure 7.4 as the least compact. In addition, one would have to decide the threshold for a particular compactness score that signals potential gerrymandering. These are relevant issues to consider since the Supreme Court has stated that any standard used for resolving claims related to partisan gerrymandering "must be grounded in a 'limited and precise rationale' and be 'clear, manageable, and politically neutral'" (*Rucho*, 2019, p. 15). For more information about using compactness metrics to identify gerrymandering, see Hofeller 2010; Kaufman et al. 2019.

The third criterion provides a different approach for identifying gerrymandered districts. It focuses on the outcome of an election based on voter distribution rather than the shape of a district. In this case, we are trying to identify maps drawn in which voters from one party have been spread out among several districts (known as cracking), or grouped together in a few districts (known as packing).

To illustrate, let us look at a different distribution of 52 X voters and 48 O voters, as shown in Figure 7.5.

In this more realistic distribution, voters of one party are concentrated in the center. If a representative from Party X wants to engage in packing and cracking, they will create a district with many voters for Party O, and spread the remaining voters among the other three districts. (See Figure 7.6.)

```
x x x x x x x x x x
x o x x o o x x o x
x x o o o o o o x x
x x o o o o o o x x
x o o o o o o o o x
x o o o o o o o o x
x x o o o o o o x x
x x o o o o o o x x
x o x x o o x x o x
x x x x x x x x x x
```

Figure 7.5. Hypothetical 52:48 Distribution of 100 Voters.

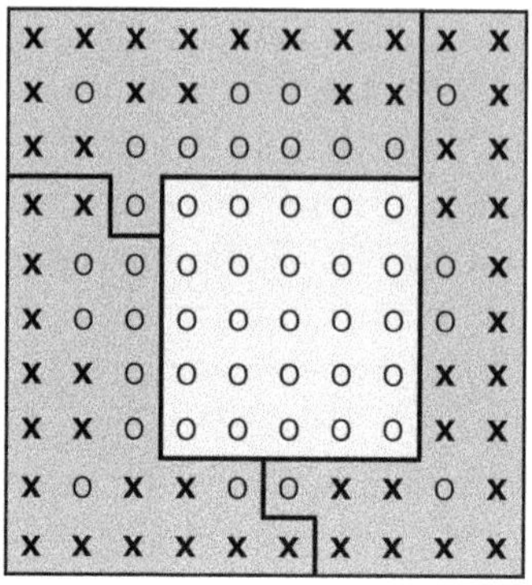

```
X X X X X X X X X X
X O X X O O X X O X
X X O O O O O O X X
X X O O O O O O X X
X O O O O O O O O X
X O O O O O O O O X
X X O O O O O O X X
X X O O O O O O X X
X O X X O O X X O X
X X X X X X X X X X
```

Figure 7.6. Map of 52:48 Distribution with Packing and Cracking.

Party X has created a situation where several districts are not competitive between the two parties. This can be quantified by finding the efficiency gap for a district map. The efficiency gap was introduced by Stephanopoulos and McGhee in 2015 and is calculated by finding the number of wasted votes for each party (Alexeev & Mixon, 2018). A wasted vote is any vote that did not contribute to a party winning its district. Since each district of Lyon contains 25 voters, a party needs at least 13 votes to win that district. Therefore, any votes after the first 13 for a party were unnecessary and considered "wasted." Likewise, all votes cast for the losing party in a district are also considered to be wasted. The efficiency gap is calculated by finding the difference between wasted votes for the two parties and expressing this difference as a percentage of the total number of voters in a state. See Table 7.3 for an example of this calculation for the district map shown in Figure 7.6.

Table 7.3. Wasted Votes in Districts in Figure 7.6

District	Votes Cast for X	Votes Cast for O	X Wasted Votes	O Wasted Votes
1	15	10	2	10
2	20	5	7	5
3	17	8	4	8
4	0	25	0	12
Total	52	48	13	35

Since Party O wasted 22 more votes than Party X (out of 100), then the efficiency gap for this particular map is 22 percent. The theoretical maximum possible efficiency gap is 50 percent and would correspond to the worst possible case of gerrymandering. Ideally an efficiency gap should be close to 0 percent. Of the maps considered so far, note the map in Figure 7.2 corresponds to the smallest efficiency gap (4%), and also has the best perimeter compactness scores. (See Table 7.4.)

However, as Figure 7.7 shows, an interesting phenomenon occurs when we try to apply this ideal district map to our new distribution of voters. Although the compactness scores are unchanged, the efficiency gap has increased to 48 percent and Party X wins all four seats. On the other hand, the map from Figure 7.4 that had the worst compactness scores now corresponds to a 4 percent efficiency gap and gives Lyon a 2–2 split between the two parties (see Figure 7.8).

It is also worth noting that a single vote changed from X to O in each district of the map of Figure 7.7 would dramatically alter the result to a 4–0 advantage for Party O. So the "cracking" of voters of Party O into all four districts could become an advantage in the future. This

Table 7.4. Efficiency Gaps of Hypothetical Districts

	Figure 7.2	Figure 7.3	Figure 7.4	Figure 7.6
Average Perimeter	1.000	0.567	0.334	0.691
Minimum Perimeter	1.000	0.391	0.207	0.476
Efficiency Gap	4%	30%	48%	22%

Figure 7.7. Compact Districts in 52:48 District.

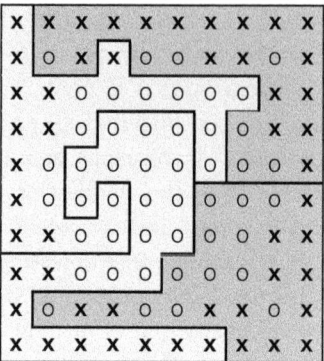

Figure 7.8. Low Efficiency Gap Districts in 52:48 District.

phenomenon was perhaps at play in an example referenced by the U.S. Supreme Court's majority opinion in *Rucho*: "Democrats also challenged the Pennsylvania congressional districting plan at issue in *Vieth*. Two years after that challenge failed, they gained four seats in the delegation, going from a 12–7 minority to an 11–8 majority. At the next election, they flipped another Republican seat" (2019, p. 24).

So one cannot assume that a high compactness score will always correspond to a low efficiency gap. In fact, Figure 7.8 shows the opposite is possible. Furthermore, Alexeev and Mixon have concluded that in some situations, "a small efficiency gap is only possible with bizarrely-shaped districts" (2018, p. 878). Specifically, they proved that every districting system will be flagged by at least one of our first three criteria (2018).

So what district map should be chosen for Lyon? We have seen that it is possible that Party X might win from one to four seats. Since compactness and efficiency gap measures give conflicting answers, we turn to another method. Criterion #4 requires simulation to find the most common outcomes for thousands of random maps. A map might be deemed "gerrymandered" if its election outcome does not fall into one of the expected distributions of seats. This is what the dissenting opinion proposed in *Rucho v Common Cause*: "Suppose now we have 1,000 maps, each with a partisan outcome attached to it. We can line up those maps on a continuum—the most favorable to Republicans on one end, the most favorable to Democrats on the other. . . . And we can see where the State's actual plan falls on the spectrum—at or near the median or way out on one of the tails?" (2019, p. 19).

Using Mathematics to Understand How Gerrymandering | 135

For our example, we randomly chose 100,000 district maps. For the sake of simplicity, these maps did not require the districts to be contiguous. While such districts might not be practical in reality, it does guarantee the most nonpartisan maps possible since "urban electoral districts are often dominated by one political party/can itself lead to inherently packed districts" (2019, p. 18). This simulation shows that for a state of 100 voters, about 54 percent of nonpartisan maps will lead to Party X winning two seats. Another 40 percent will yield three seats to Party X, while 5 percent will give Party X one seat. Thus, one could argue that any map for Lyon leading to party X winning one or four seats should be flagged for partisan gerrymandering.

This result seems to match our intuition for "fairness" based on the proportion of X voters to O voters. However, this intuition is shattered when the parameters for a state are tweaked. As Table 7.5 shows, the expected distribution of seats quickly changes if the advantage of the majority party increases. These simulations show that even if 40 percent of Lyon votes for Party O, more often than not a random map will result in Party X winning all four seats. This outcome is all but guaranteed if the proportion of Party O voters drops to less than 30 percent.

7.5. Number of Votes out of 100 for Party X

Seats won by X	Number of votes out of 100 for Party X					
	50	52	55	60	65	70
1	17%	5%	0%	0%	0%	0%
2	66%	54%	24%	2%	0%	0%
3	17%	40%	63%	43%	14%	3%
4	0%	1%	13%	54%	86%	97%

7.6. Seats Won by X in 52:48 Distribution with 100, 1,000, and 10,000 Voters[6]

Seats won by X	100 voters	1000 voters	10,000 voters
1	5%	0%	0%
2	54%	19%	0%
3	40%	64%	5%
4	1%	17%	95%

---

6. Due to time constraints, only 10,000 simulations were created for a population of 1,000 voters, and 1,000 simulations for a population of 10,000 voters.

These trends become more pronounced as the population of a state increases. As Table 7.6 indicates, even a slim 52 percent majority will eventually guarantee that Party X wins all four seats if the population is large enough. This fact was recognized by the majority opinion in *Rucho* quoting Justice White: "[i]f all or most of the districts are competitive . . . even a narrow statewide preference for either party would produce an overwhelming majority for the winning party in the state legislature" (as cited in 2019, p. 18). So although Criterion #4 gives another nonpartisan approach for investigating gerrymandering, the conclusion one reaches through simulation may not be satisfying if one feels representation should be approximately proportional.

A more sophisticated simulation will generate different results. The fact that states generally do not have all their districts vote in favor of a single party indicates that contiguousness of districts affects the outcome. In other words, party affiliation is not randomly distributed across a state. Thus, the minority party is likely to have enough votes concentrated in one region of a state to win at least one district. Simulations that take into account contiguousness, county lines, or other state-specific restrictions will be less random and more likely benefit the minority party.

For example, let us simulate the district boundaries for Iowa. Like Lyon, Iowa is divided into four districts, and in the 2016 election, approximately 52.2 percent of the 1.6 million voters chose the Republican Donald Trump for president (McDonald, 2018). As we have already seen, if those voters were randomly divided into four equal groups, we would expect all four districts to vote Republican, even if all of the remaining 47.8 percent of voters chose a Democratic candidate. This would occur for almost every possible simulated district map.

However, it is not practical to randomly place voters in districts. In Iowa, county lines are used for district boundaries. Thus, our simulation simplifies to dividing the 99 counties into four groups. To make our simulation more realistic, we will only allow district configurations that are contiguous and keep the population of each within 50,000 of the other three districts. Also, we will consider the proportion of voters for each county that voted for Trump, and the turnout percentage for each county. For simplicity, we will assume all people who voted for Trump will vote Republican, and those that did not will vote for a Democrat. Figure 7.9 shows examples of all possible outcomes and Table 7.7 shows the results of more than 1,000 simulations.

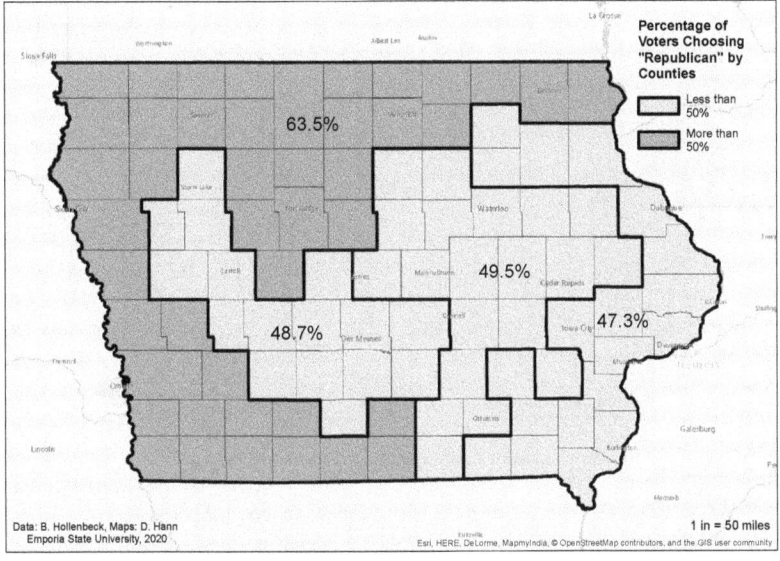

Figure 7.9a. Iowa Map with 3–1 Democratic Advantage, 2016.

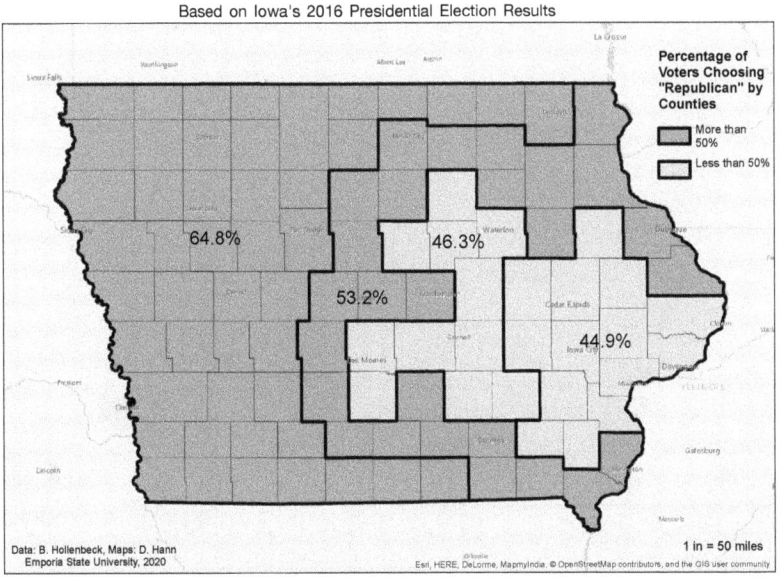

Figure 7.9b. Iowa Map with 2–2 Split, 2016.

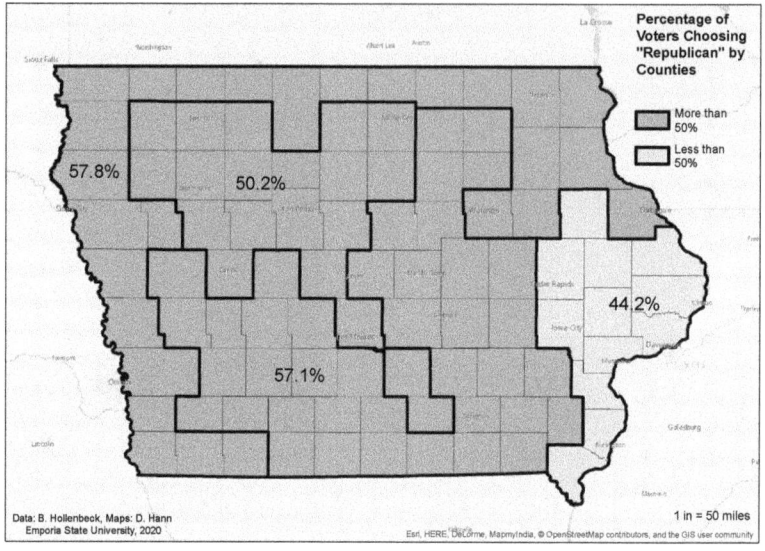

Figure 7.9c. Iowa Map with 3–1 Republican Advantage, 2016.

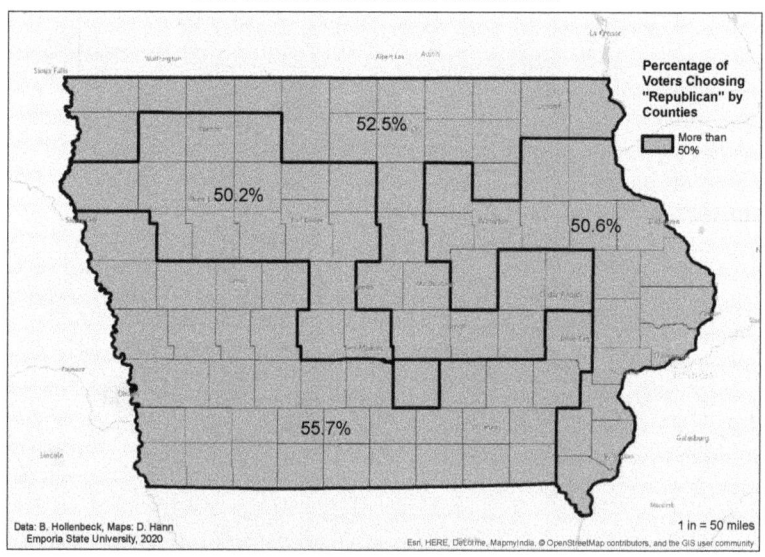

Figure 7.9d. Iowa Map with 4–0 Republican Advantage, 2016.

7.7. Results of 1,000 Districting Simulations for Iowa, 2016

Seats Won by Republicans	Percentage of District Maps
0	0%
1	9.4%
2	80.8%
3	9.8%
4	0.1%

Notice that the extra conditions dramatically change the results of the simulation. While the most nonpartisan and "fair" distribution of voters will almost always give Republicans a 4–0 advantage, the artificial constraints of county lines and contiguousness result in a 2–2 split for 81 percent of the simulations.

For another example, consider the 13 congressional districts of North Carolina. In the 2016 election, 49.8 percent of voters selected the Republican nominee for president while 46.2 percent chose the Democratic nominee. Despite this slim difference, ten of 13 districts voted Republican. Using the given percentages from 2016, suppose we assign each of North Carolina's 2,706 precincts a voter preference—Republican, Democrat, or neither. We next randomly distribute those precincts into 13 districts of approximately the same number of precincts. We repeat this experiment 1,000 times. Table 7.8 shows the results of this simulation, assuming any tied districts went equally to Republicans and Democrats. Notice about 40 percent of these maps will result in Republicans winning at least 10 seats. On the other hand, a less random simulation conducted by an expert witness that takes into account North Carolina districting criteria had zero maps out of 3,000 give Republicans a 10–3 advantage or better (*Rucho*, 2019).

7.8. Results of 3,000 Hypothetical Maps for North Carolina, 2016

# of districts won by Republicans	7 or less	8	9	10	11 or more
% of maps	5%	18%	36%	30%	10%

Conclusion

Mathematics provides several tools to help us quantify vague concerns such as a strangely shaped district or an outcome that skews against our intuition of what is fair or right. However, controversy remains because there are philosophical questions that must be answered first. For example, is proportional representation a desirable goal? As the majority opinion pointed out in *Rucho*: "The Founders certainly did not think proportional representation was required. For more than 50 years after the ratification of the Constitution, many States elected their congressional representatives through at-large or "general ticket" elections. Such States typically sent single-party delegations to Congress" (2019, p. 16). They also point out that political gerrymandering is allowed up to a point. The real question is to determine when "political gerrymandering has gone too far" (2019, p. 2).

On the other hand, the dissenting opinion says proportional representation or "fairness" is not the point at all. Their viewpoint is "manipulation of district lines for partisan gain" should be eliminated (2019, p. 25). From this perspective, a deviation from a nonpartisan norm should be avoided. Through simulation, mathematics can also provide insight for this standard. But one must first decide what is considered "normal" and what deviation is too much. For example, Maryland has been cited as an egregious example of partisan gerrymandering. Officials admitted they redrew the map to change the Democrats' advantage over the Republicans from 6–2 to 7–1 (*Rucho*, 2019). However, in 100 percent of random, nonpartisan maps simulated at the precinct level, Democrats received an 8–0 advantage. This outcome actually models the situation in Massachusetts, which has a similar ratio of Democrats and Republicans. Democrats routinely win all congressional seats since Republicans are "cracked" among all the districts. Should the distribution of voters for a party determine the outcome of an election, or only the number of voters for that party? That question must be answered before mathematics can be used to solve issues related to gerrymandering.

References

Alexeev, B., & Mixon, D. (2018). An impossibility theorem for gerrymandering. *The American Mathematical Monthly*, *125*(10), 878–884.

Azavea Redistricting. (2019). How do we know if gerrymandering has occurred?
Davis v. Bandemer 478 US 109 (1986).
Hofeller, T. (2010). Compactness in the redistricting process. https://www.ncsl.org/Documents/legismgt/Compactness-Hofeller.pdf.
Kaufman, A., King, G., & Komisarchik, M. (2019). How to measure legislative district compactness if you only know it when you see it. http://j.mp/2u9OWrG.
McDonald, M. 2018. (2016). November general election turnout rates. http://www.electproject.org/2016g.
Miller v. Johnson 515 US 900 (1995).
Rucho v. Common Cause. No. 18-422, 588 U. S. ____ (2019).

Chapter 8

Civil Rights Groups Respond

Kevin Anderson

Introduction

The central question in a democratic government is, How are citizens' preferences translated into public policy? Voting as an essential right in a democratic polity is a fundamental element of self-government, and for minority groups access to the ballot is critical to not only basic tenets of democracy but to the protection of rights relative to the majority within their society. How can minorities that historically have been discriminated against and have had to fight for full access to all the rights of full citizenship, respond to policy changes that might create obstacles to the ballot box and that, in context, might complicate other aspects of their everyday life?

Over the course of American history, the response of civil rights groups and their allies can be roughly grouped into three categories. The *legislative* strategy is focused on changing the law, for example, the Civil Rights Act of 1965. The *legal* strategy focuses on seeking redress through the courts. This includes a series of rulings by the U.S. Supreme Court and lower courts declaring various state laws and practices unconstitutional, and it started well before the heyday of the civil rights era in the 1950s and 1960s. Finally, the *protest* strategy focuses on using protest as a means of building support and pressing for change. It is exemplified in the work of Dr. Martin Luther King Jr., and the civil rights movement of the 1960s. Today the BlackLivesMatter movement has engaged on this front and represents a new perspective on voting rights in contemporary politics.

Historical Strategic Responses

African Americans have employed numerous tactics to secure and maintain access to the ballot box. At the core of each of these strategies is both an argument for the protection of the individual right to vote as essential to citizenship and the idea of perfecting democratic government in America. The earliest protest actions against voter exclusion rested on the idea of disenfranchisement as a violation of individual liberty inherent in denying citizens the right to vote. Over time, this concern was married to a broader argument that voter exclusion undermined the core idea of democratic government. These two principles helped define the strategic choices of those fighting for the elective franchise. The passage of Thirteenth, Fourteenth, and Fifteenth Amendments after the Civil War during the Reconstruction era created new opportunities for political activism. The Union Leagues, originally founded in Northern states during the Civil War to support the war effort, began organizing in the South to boost the new amendments by helping to register and mobilize voters in Southern cities, such as Richmond, Raleigh, and Nashville (Hahn, 2003). The work of these groups helped to undergird the first sustained government action taken to bring African Americans into the political arena. The ability of the national government to act on behalf of a formally excluded population established a pattern in which the goal of political activism for some within the newly freed population is to organize and use the national government to force the entire nation (specifically, state governments) to extend individual rights to all citizens. To define political rights in general, and access to the ballot specifically, as a national concern became a key aspect of the new African American political class.

The adoption of the Fifteenth Amendment guaranteeing all men the right to vote in 1870 led to the federal government adopting a strong oversight role in protecting that right. In a striking historical parallel, Congress passed the "Enforcement Acts" of 1870 and 1871. Also known as the "Ku Klux Klan" acts, these were four laws designed to protect the rights of newly enfranchised voters in the South that granted the federal courts and the president the power to punish anyone who interfered with another person's right to vote based on race, gender, or previous condition of servitude. These laws established the federal government as an essential level of protection against state level discrimination (Smith et al., 2014). They also established a historical precursor to the preclearance provision of the 1965 Voting Rights Act that was struck down by the Roberts Supreme Court in the 2013 case *Shelby County v Holder*.

The early fights for maintaining access to the ballot after the rollback of Reconstruction and the numerous state laws that undermined the Fifteenth Amendment, are chronicled by R. Volney Riser in his book *Defying Disenfranchisement*, where he points out that the focus of early litigation was on the *intent* of state laws passed rather on the results on those laws. If state voting laws could be defended as neutral on the question of race, then legal remedies had a limited efficacy; thus, the need to maintain a strong role for the federal government. The 1875 Supreme Court case *Minor v Happersett* is illustrative of the point. In this case, the court ruled that a Missouri woman was a citizen of the state, however her status as a citizen did not guarantee her the right to vote because state law in Missouri did not recognize the right of women to vote. This decision proved the necessity for federal action to protect access to the ballot because the court upheld a state court decision in which Missouri declared who had the right to vote and who did not. The impact of this ruling, returning the power of determining voter eligibility to the states, undercut the power of the federal government to use the Enforcement Acts as a way of guaranteeing African Americans the right to vote (Riser, 2010).

The passage of new state laws regarding voting was ostensibly to protect the "sanctity" of the electoral process. For example, the Dortch law was one of several passed in Tennessee in 1889. It defined specific punishments for anyone "assisting" illiterate, ill-informed, or confused voters in any of the state's four urban counties. Tennessee also passed the Myers law, requiring voters to register twenty days before every election in any community with more than 500 voters, and the Lea law, which provided separate ballot boxes for state and federal elections. In 1893, South Carolina passed voter reform legislation requiring that voters must register and provide proof that they had voted in all elections since they had reached legal voting age dating back to 1857. In 1893, Mississippi attorney general Wiley Nash argued that the collection of poll taxes might net the state up to $500,000 annually, revenue the state could not afford to lose.

The arguments behind such legislation and other more well-known mechanisms such as literacy tests, grandfather clauses, and poll taxes were all described as deterrents to fraud and necessary for a healthy democracy. Literacy tests and poll taxes were replacements for the idea of landowners being the only legitimate voters because their property could be taxed, and therefore they would be most likely to pay close attention to politics. Philosophically understood and divorced from their racial implications, landowner requirements, literacy tests, and poll taxes all reflected the idea that to vote one needed "skin in the game." If you had property at risk of being taxed, you deserved the opportunity to select the government officials who would decide on those taxes (Smith et al., 2014). These laws all pivoted on the idea of a "worthy" voter casting legitimate ballots. How can we elect good candidates and pass legitimate public policy if we have uninformed voters with no history of civic activity casting ballots?

African American leaders, however, instead of arguing that safeguards were needed to prevent fraudulent votes, began arguing that the real fraud was exclusion of black voters; In their eyes, this delegitimized election results in the affected states. In 1921, W. E. B. Du Bois powerfully captured this point. Editorializing in *The Crisis*, the official magazine of the National Association for the Advancement of Colored People (NAACP), he wrote:

> Moreover, states can easily disenfranchise a whole group by choosing certain characteristics or disabilities of the group: Negroes as a mass are poor and ignorant; a property and literacy qualification will therefore disenfranchise a large number of them. . . . Hitherto democracy in the United States has assumed that self-interest would keep the numbers of voters as large as possible in various states. This assumption has failed in two respects: It has kept women from voting for more than a century and it has kept Negroes in the South from voting for the better part of a generation. . . . The Constitution does not attempt to say that the state may not have perfectly good moral ground for such disenfranchisement. In sheer self-defense it may be proper, temporarily, for a state

to disenfranchise the ignorant. It might even defend itself, under a just economic system, in disenfranchising the poor. (Du Bois, 1921)

The editorial goes on to argue that if a state acts to remove citizens from the voting rolls, then the state should have a resulting reduction in the number of members in its congressional delegation; again, if democracy is the core principle, then any changes to the voting system must enhance access to the ballot. Once states began to pass laws such as grandfather clauses, poll taxes, and literacy tests, the legal strategy necessary to challenge these laws needed to evolve since these laws did not expressly mention race as a factor in the restrictions they imposed. This led to voting rolls that changed dramatically in numerous states; between 1896 and 1904 Louisiana lost 130,000 black voters, Virginia went from 147,000 black voters to 21,000, and by 1906 Alabama's share of black voters was down to 2 percent (May, 2013).

The right to vote is not defined as an explicit right in the Constitution of the United States; the power to determine who votes has historically been defined by individual states. While civil rights advocates debated many different approaches, NAACP leadership ultimately settled on a strategy of legal action (Anderson, 2010). This meant a series of cases forcing the courts to confront myriad state laws and complex eligibility requirements. The United States Supreme Court ultimately issued a trio of legal decisions that addressed major barriers to the franchise and helped enunciate voting as an essential right.

In the 1941 case, *United States v Classic*, the Court, in addressing a question involving voting in a party primary, affirmed the right to vote as a vital aspect of citizenship by stating that Congress did have the right to regulate party primaries if they were essential to the democratic process of selecting political representation. In other words, if a political party is dominant in a state, its primary could serve as tantamount to an election and barring voters from the primary was an infringement upon their right to cast a meaningful ballot. In later affirming the one-man one-vote principle in the 1964 case of *Reynolds v Sims*, the Court once again defended the right to vote by striking down Alabama state legislative districts that were apportioned in such a way as to dilute the voting power of individual voters by grouping minority voters in one district and allowing other districts to be much more dispersed, thereby allowing some voters much more influence over their elected representatives than others.

In striking down the poll tax, in the 1966 case *Harper v Virginia State Board of Elections*, the court noted the fundamental importance of voting and struck down a policy that conditioned the right to vote on the payment of a tax or a fee as a violation of the Equal Protection Clause of the Fourteenth Amendment. The court deemed this action as a barrier to citizen participation in the polity and noted that: "The interest of the state when it comes to voter registration is limited to fixing of standards related to applicant's qualification as a voter" (*Harper v Virginia State Board of Elections*, 1966). In each of these cases, the court found that state actions must protect the right to vote, and that any policies that interfere with this right must meet the established legal standard,

In the twentieth century, the formal legal barriers put in place through state restrictions such as grandfather clauses and literacy tests were supplemented by the tactic of "voter caging." The practice of caging, a term borrowed from direct mail advertising campaigns, involves non-forwardable mail being sent to a list of voters. If the mail is returned as undeliverable, that is used as proof that the addressee is ineligible to vote or may be attempting to commit voter fraud. This tactic drew renewed attention following a congressional investigation into the allegedly partisan firing of United States attorneys in 2007, however, it has a long history of being employed as a way of suppressing minority voters.

A report by Project Vote noted the history of the caging tactic, with detailed descriptions of operations in 1958 in Arizona, 1981 in New Jersey, 1986 in Louisiana, and 1990 in North Carolina. However, the most comprehensive version of this tactic was the 1964 Operation Eagle Eye campaign run by the Republican National Committee in the wake of the election of John F. Kennedy in a close race over Richard Nixon in 1960, an election some Republicans felt had been stolen. This led to a national caging strategy run by Harlington Wood for the Republican National Committee. This strategy was challenged legally in court and politically by Democratic operatives (who used a version of the tactic themselves in later elections), yet it continued to be a way to target voters who were thought to be committing voter fraud. It drew renewed attention after the 2004 presidential election, as Ohio, Florida, Pennsylvania, and Wisconsin all saw versions of this tactic embraced by Republicans and challenged by Democrats in a tight presidential race in several swing states. The 2004 litigation on voter challenge laws (and the caging that was part of the voter challenge laws) resulted in many of the restrictive new laws ultimately being upheld by the U.S. Supreme Court (Project Vote, 2007). A further challenge to the voter rules was passed in the state of Ohio, to allow voters to be purged from the rolls if they have not voted in two years and a state-mailed notice is not returned within four years. The state's stance was upheld in 2018 in the case *Husted v A. Phillip Randolph Institute*. This decision along with the ruling by the Roberts Court in 2013 harkens back to the legal justifications for the *Minor* ruling and creates a new (old) line of argument for litigation surrounding voting rights.

Voting Rights in Contemporary Politics

In the leadup to the 2018 congressional elections, access to the ballot became a key issue in two high-profile races for governor in the states of Georgia and Florida. Stacey Abrams, the Democratic nominee in Georgia, accused her opponent, Secretary of State Brian Kemp, of engaging in voter suppression through the delay in certifying 53,000 new voter registrations as well as declaring more than 3,000 voters ineligible to vote (they were later shown to be eligible). The close margin of the race, (Kemp won the race 50.2 percent versus Abrams's 48.8percent) intensified the questions about how Secretary Kemp did his job as secretary of state and led Abrams to join Fair Fight Action, a group dedicated to election reform and voter education.

In Florida, Tallahassee mayor Democrat Andrew Gillum launched a historic campaign for governor against Republican Ron DeSantis and along with the attention his race received due to his status as the first African American nominee for governor in the history of the state, media coverage also focused on Amendment 4; The Voting Rights Restoration for Felons Initiative. If approved by voters, this new law that would reinstate the right to vote for persons with felony convictions after they had served their sentence in prison and completed any probation. This was the most overt attempted expansion of voting rights in the country during the fall elections and the question of whether it would pass, combined with its very public support by Mayor Gillum, drew a sharp spotlight to the Florida election.

Amendment 4 passed with 65 percent of the vote, yet political considerations were still in play as the state legislature continued debating how to implement the law in 2019. A set of proposed changes created sharp partisan divisions; a proposal to make sure that all fines and fees associated with conviction are paid before the right to vote is restored passed in a Florida House committee on a party line vote, with Republicans supporting the change and Democrats opposing the change and labeling it a "modern day poll tax" and thus an impediment to voting. The proposal also passed the state senate and the legislation was signed into law by Governor DeSantis in June 2019 (Mower and Mahoney, 2019). In May 2020, the law was struck down by United States District Court judge Robert Hinkle who described it as a violation of the Twenty-Fourth Amendment.

The Democratic Party won back control of the United States House of Representatives in the 2018 congressional election and among their legislative priorities was the Voting Rights Advancement Act of 2019. Introduced in the House of Representatives by Terri Sewell of Alabama and introduced in the Senate by Patrick Leahy of Vermont, the bill currently had 192 co-sponsors and was touted as an essential part of the party agenda in Congress. The introduction of this bill has induced lobbying efforts from a wide spectrum of interest groups, from organizations that have historically fought for civil rights, such as the National Association for the Advancement of Colored People (NAACP) and the Urban League, to modern civil rights groups such as Human Rights Campaign, Transformative Justice Coalition, and Public Citizen. Their lobbying efforts are national in scope and grassroots in implementation and while the goal of expanding voting rights is broadly shared, the specific goals of each organization create a varied and comprehensive base of support for voting reform. The Democrats won control of both houses of Congress and the presidency in 2020 and have introduced a more comprehensive bill, the For the People Act, in 2021 and the debate over the law remains as partisan as earlier efforts at voter reform. The methods of activism around voting reform have traditionally split into two strategic options: litigation and social movement activities. Traditional pluralist interest groups may seek to use both strategies given the varied nature of the issue and the resources of the particular group.

Strategic Response One: Modern Litigation

Once new voting laws were passed after the 2013 *Shelby* decision, several lawsuits were filed, and among the most notable groups participating was the National Association for the Advancement of Colored People

(NAACP). The organization has a long history of litigation in this area, including winning the 1944 court case *Smith v Allwright*, which outlawed the all-white primary in the state of Texas. The NAACP and its legal arm, the NAACP Legal Defense Fund (LDF) utilized a legal approach that was versatile enough to object to the general idea of these new voting laws while also filing other lawsuits targeting their specific provisions. In each of these cases, the lead plaintiff represented minority communities that argued that these laws undermined access to the ballot thus setting up a legal debate involving the Voting Rights Act of 1965. What are reasonable restrictions that the state can impose on voting? Are these restrictions in violation of the right to vote as guaranteed by the Voting Rights Act of 1965? The legal arguments in each of these cases placed the burden of proof on the state to prove that the new requirements did not impose great barriers to access to the ballot. This approach meant that if plaintiffs could illustrate (measured through demographic analysis) that the new laws had a disparate impact on a community, that is, the *effect* of the laws rather than their intent, which had been the focus of earlier litigation, then these laws violated the 1965 Voting Rights Act which some argue provided legal protection of access to the ballot box.

In North Carolina, the Obama Justice Department joined with several civil rights organizations (Including the League of Women Voters) to contest a 2013 law passed by the state legislature in the wake of *Shelby v Holder*. *North Carolina v State Conference of the NAACP et al.* (16-833 2017), a case growing out of an earlier challenge, *North Carolina NAACP v McCrory*, was a broad-based challenge that focused on the drawing of congressional district lines, the types of identification acceptable to vote, limitations on early voting, the elimination of same-day registration, and the preregistration of some teenagers within one year of their being eligible to vote. The Fourth Circuit Court of Appeals ruled against the state law in 2016, arguing that "the challenged provisions were enacted with racially discriminatory intent in violation of the Equal Protection Clause of the 14th Amendment and Section 2 of the Voting Rights Act" (*North Carolina v McCrory 831 F. 3d 204 [4th Circuit 2016]*), and the Supreme Court in 2017 refused to revive the law, citing confusion over who had the legal right to seek review of the Fourth Circuit Court's ruling.

A similar dynamic occurred in Texas, with a new voter identification law going into effect in 2013 that was immediately challenged by the Texas State Conference of the NAACP and the Mexican American Legislative Caucus. The case, *Texas NAACP v Steen* consolidated with

Veasey v Steen (also known as *Veasey v Perry*), challenged voter identification requirements, specifically the types of identification that were acceptable; (concealed carry permits were valid, university student identification cards were not). The plaintiffs argued that the law, by creating a disparate impact on minority voters, violated Section 2 of the Voting Rights Act. The law was overturned in a ruling by Judge Nelva Gonzales Ramos of the United States Southern District Court of Texas in April 2017. In the opinion, Judge Ramos noted:

> To call SB 14's disproportionate impact on minorities statistically significant would be an understatement. Dr. Ansolabehere's ecological regression analysis found that African American registered voters were 305% more likely and Hispanic registered voters 195% more likely than Anglo registered voters to lack SB 14 qualified ID. (*Veasey v Perry*, 769 F. 3d 890 [2014])

In each of these cases, the foundation of opposition rested on the illustration of disproportionate effects without any type of immediate remediation, thus serving as an evolution from the earlier legal strategy of trying to prove discriminatory *intent* in the language of the law. A North Dakota voter identification law, first passed in 2004 and challenged by the Turtle Mountain Band of Chippewa and argued by the Native American Rights Fund in *Brakebill et al. v Jaeger*, was blocked in 2016. However, when United States District Court judge Daniel Hovland blocked the law, he allowed a provision requiring voters who lacked the designated identification to sign affidavits swearing that they were legal voters, thus allowing challenged voters to cast a ballot. This ruling considered the claims of voter fraud by allowing a way to verify the status of voters that was not deemed to be burdensome to the right to vote. These legal arguments provided one front of opposition to the new voting laws, including extensive litigation in Kansas and Georgia, that reflected the general theme of argument outlined above, but they were not the only strategy of resistance for those opposed to these new laws.

Strategic Response Two: Social Movements and Voting

The understanding of voting as an essential part of citizenship implies a moral argument to protect access to the ballot that becomes an important part of the next type of opposition to voting laws: political resistance. When one party controls the legislative branch of state government and can determine both congressional and state district boundaries as well as defining the actual process for voting, the claims of unfair political gamesmanship will come quickly and loudly. The arguments in favor of and against these laws soon took on the frame of one party accusing the other of unethical intent, ulterior motives, undemocratic behavior. What did this political argument look like?

The nature of voter identification laws lends itself to a model of resistance that relies on legal challenges, yet social movement–style protest and pluralist lobbying strategies are also employed. One of the most notable of these tactics was the Moral Mondays protest in North Carolina led by the president of the state chapter of the NAACP, William Barber. The protest rallies at the state capital in Raleigh constituted a program of resistance to a wide range of issues, from voting rights to a living wage, yet the framing of access to the ballot as a fundamentally moral issue created pressure on the legislature, who were lobbied to repeal the law by the state NAACP. These rallies soon sparked increased activism by other North Carolina groups such as the Southern Coalition of Social Justice, which provided legal services and community organizing against the North Carolina voting law, as well as the ACLU, which fully engaged on the legal front by joining in litigation and issuing legal analysis of the laws passed by the state legislature which had helped sparked the protest rallies (Barber & Wilson-Hartgrove, 2016).

In Texas, litigation was an important part of resistance; however, political resistance did not center on the African American community. The social movement protest did involve the NAACP, but other groups such as the League of United Latin American Citizens (LULAC), the Justice Seekers, and the Texas Association of Hispanic County Judges and Commissioners all were actively engaged in political activity surrounding the right to vote. This broader coalition advocated for issues far beyond the technical aspects of the law. The resistance to voter identification laws reflected a broader sense of isolation among these communities; questions of language restrictions and access to the ballot, the role of voting in defining citizenship, and the political questions that surround immigration, education, and crime have animated the protests these groups engage in. The recent conflicts over immigration policy inspired by the Trump administration at the border, and especially by family separations, has raised the stakes on citizenship and voting and became a key issue heading into the 2020 presidential election. These issues help to explain why these groups protest and what these groups seek beyond the right to vote. The lobbying against voter identification laws was not just tied to a moral argument about democracy (although that was important) but was directly connected to policy outcomes in other parts of life that are directly relevant to day-to-day life.

Modern social protest movements have coalesced around issues such as economic inequality and police reform among African Americans and has led to the formation of social justice groups such as Black Lives Matter. Although the focus of the group is on police reform, voting rights are viewed as essential to bolstering their overall goal. In the state of Missouri, after the conflagration in Ferguson following the death of Michael Brown, voting was perceived as one of the vital tools needed to reverse the perceived exploitation and oppression of the local government. The Justice Department released a report in 2015 detailing how the city appeared to be attempting to maximize revenue through arrests, fines, and fees on the citizens, thus, monetizing the criminal justice system rather than simply enforcing the law, became a source of revenue for the city. The act of voting became a way of addressing criminal justice issues directly as a political issue and possibly correcting an everyday consequence of ethically compromised public policy.

The focus on criminal justice after numerous police shootings led to several high-profile victories for candidates viewed as progressive on the criminal justice issues. In Baltimore, after the death of Freddie Gray in police custody, Baltimore State's Attorney Marilyn Mosby quickly filed charges against city police officers involved in his arrest and injury in custody; however, none of the officers charged was convicted and there is ongoing litigation regarding wrongful prosecution. However, the decision to indict was popular at the time among community activists. In Chicago, Kim Foxx defeated Anita Alvarez for the Cook County State's Attorney position after the controversial handling of the LaQuan McDonald case in 2016. In Philadelphia, Larry Krasner, a career defense attorney who had sued city police 75 times, was elected as the next Philadelphia District Attorney in 2017. In Georgia in 2018, Lucy McBath won a congressional seat in the Sixth District, campaigning on the issue of gun control after the murder of her seventeen-year-old son Jordan Davis following a dispute with a white motorist over the volume of his music. Lesley McSpadden, the mother of Michael Brown, the young man killed in Ferguson, Missouri, became an activist and author and ran for the Ferguson City Council on a reform of the criminal justice system platform, and although she did not win (she finished third in the race), she remains an advocate for the changes in Ferguson.

The most notable political victories from the era of Black Lives Matter occurred in St. Louis in 2018 where Wesley Bell defeated Bob McCullough in an election for St. Louis County Prosecutor. After the unrest in Ferguson, a movement to change city and county government led to the upset of the seven-term incumbent who failed to file charges against Darren Wilson in the killing of Michael Brown in 2014. Fueled by a grassroots campaign and a popular social media hashtag (#BYEBOB), Bell scored a fourteen-point victory in the Democratic primary. After taking office, he has stopped imposing cash bail for misdemeanor charges and created a unit to investigate past convictions, among a host of reforms that speak to the community concerns that helped get him elected. He has also replaced a few staff attorneys who did not aggressively pursue accusations of police misconduct under the previous administration. Cori Bush, a St. Louis Registered Nurse and activist involved in the Black Lives Matter movement challenged 1st Congressional District incumbent Democrat Congressman Lacy Clay in 2020 and won a surprise victory in the primary. She is an active supporter of the For the People Act and introduced an amendment to the act expanding access to Dropbox for voters, which passed the House of Representatives and is under consideration in the Senate.

Conclusion

The nature of voting as an essential element of American democracy means that even simple, technical changes to the process provoke debate regarding the morality and political implications of any such changes. Historian Carol Anderson argues that the fight over voting rights reflects an ongoing series of challenges along racial, economic, and social fronts. The number of states pursuing changes in recent years has led to an intense resistance that has tried to block these changes through lawsuits, lobbying, and public pressure, joined by civil rights groups that have engaged in resistance using strategies and tactics that have historically created significant change in American politics.

The use of litigation to challenge the legal and technical changes in voting laws is an evolving strategy built on the lessons of past legal fights over access to the ballot, and the pressure tactics of social movements lend a moral and partisan flavor to the fight, yet the essence of the issue remains protecting the most important right of citizens in a democracy: the right to vote.

References

Anderson, C. (2018). *One person, No vote: How voter suppression is destroying our democracy.* Bloomsbury.
Anderson, K. (2010). *Agitations: Ideologies and strategies in African American politics.* University of Arkansas Press.
Barber, W., & Wilson-Hartgrove, J. (2016). *The third reconstruction: Moral Mondays, fusion politics, and the rise of a new justice movement.* Beacon Press.
Berman, A. (2011). The GOP war on voting. *Rolling Stone.* August 30.
Brakebill v. Jaeger 508 US _____ (2018).
Burden, B., Canon, D., Mayer, K., & Moynihan, D. (2014). Election laws, mobilization, and turnout: The unanticipated consequences of election reform. *American Journal of Political Science, 58*(1), 95–109.
Cambell, A., Converse, P., Miller, W., & and Stokes, D. (1980). *The American voter.* University of Chicago Press.
Colby, D. (1986). The Voting Rights Act and Black registration in Mississippi. *Publius, 16*(4), 123–137.
Crawford v. Marion County Election Board 553 US 181 (2008).
Davidson, C., Dunlap, T., Kenney, D., & Wise, B. (2008). Vote caging as a Republican ballot security technique. *William Mitchell Law Review, 34*(2).
Du Bois, W. (1921). Reduced representation in Congress. *The Crisis, 21*(4).
Fullerton, A., & Casey Borch, C. (2008). Reconsidering explanations for regional convergence in voter registration and turnout in the United States, 1956–2000. *Sociological Forum, 23*(4), 755–785.
Hahn, S. (2003). *A nation under our feet: Black political struggles in the rural South from slavery to the Great Migration.* Belknap Press.
Hamer, M. (2007). An alternative approach to estimating who is most likely to respond to changes in registration laws. *Political Behavior, 29*(1), 1–30.
Harper v. Virginia State Board of Elections 383 U.S. 663 (1966).
Husted v. A Philip Randolph Institute 16-980 584 U.S. (2018).
James, T. (2007). Caging democracy: A 50-year history of partisan challenges to minority voters. A Project Vote Report.
Jones v. DeSantis 410 F. Supp. 3rd 1284 (2019).
King, J. (1994). Political culture, registration laws, and voter turnout among the American states. *Publius, 24*(4), 115–127.
Levitt, J. (2007). The truth about voter fraud. New York University: Brennan Institute of Justice.

Lipton, E., & Urbina, I. (2007). In 5-year effort, scant evidence of voter fraud. *The New York Times*. April 12.
May, G. (2013). *Bending toward justice: The Voting Rights Act and the transformation of American democracy*. Basic Books.
McDonald, M. (2008). Portable voter registration. *Political Behavior, 30*(4), 491–501.
Michelson, M. (2003). Getting out the Latino vote: How door-to-door canvassing influences voter turnout in rural Central California. *Political Behavior, 25*(3), 247–263.
Minor V. Happersett 88 U.S. (21 Wall.) 162 (1875).
Mitchell, G., & Wlezien, C. (1995). The impact of legal constraints on voter registration, turnout, and the composition of the American electorate. *Political Behavior, 17*(2), 179–202.
Mower, L., & Mahoney, E. (2019). House passes Amendment 4 bill requiring felons to pay up before they can vote. *Miami Herald*. April 24.
Murphy, D. (2019). Wesley Bell creating unit to investigate past convictions in St. Louis County. *Riverfront Times*. June 25.
Nagler, J. (1991). The effect of registration laws and education on U.S. voter turnout. *American Political Science Review, 85*(4), 1393–1405.
National Conference of State Legislatures. (2014). Voter Identification Requirements | Voter ID Laws.
North Carolina v. State Conference of the NAACP et al. 16-833 (2017).
North Carolina v. McCory 831 F. 3d 204 4th Circuit (2016).
Piven, F., & Cloward, R. (1996). Northern Bourbons: A preliminary report on the National Voter Registration Act. *PS Political Science and Politics, 29*(1), 39–42.
Ramirez, R. (2005). Giving voice to Latino voters: A field experiment on the effectiveness of a national nonpartisan mobilization effort. *Annals of American Academy of Political and Social Science, 601*, 66–84.
Reynolds v. Sims 377 U.S. 533 (1964).
Riser, R. (2010). *Defying disfranchisement: Black voting rights activism in the Jim Crow South 1890–1908*. Louisiana State University Press.
Rosenstone, S., & Wolfinger, R. (1978). The effect of registration laws on voter turnout. *American Political Science Review, 72*(1), 22–45.
Schultz, D. (2007). Less than fundamental: The myth of voter fraud and the coming of the second Great Disenfranchisement. *William Mitchell Law Review, 34*, 484–532.
Shelby County v. Holder 570 US 529 (2013).
Sides, J., & Vavrek, L. (2013). *The gamble: Choice and chance in the 2012 presidential election*. Princeton University Press.
Smith, M., Anderson, K., & Rackaway, C. (2014). *State voting laws in America: Historical statutes and their modern implication*. Palgrave Pivot.
Smith v. Allrwight 321 US 529 (1944).

Sterling, C. (1983). Time-off laws and voter turnout. *Polity, 16*(1), 143–149.
United States v. Classic 313 U.S. 299 (1941).
Veasey v. Perry 769 F 3d 890 (2014).
Vedlitz, A. (1985). Registration drives and Black voting in the South. *Journal of Politics, 47*(2), 643–651.
Wolfinger, R., & Rosenstone, S. (1980). *Who votes?* Yale University Press.

Conclusion

Michael A. Smith and Chapman Rackaway

Expanding and Contracting the Franchise

The modern-day laws that restrict rather than expand the franchise can be subsumed under six general intents: requiring prospective voter registrants to provide proof of citizenship, mandating that prospective voters provide photo identification, limiting the voting rights of those convicted of felonies, culling voting registries through "caging," redrawing districts in ways that many people call gerrymandering, and finally, changing the mechanics of voting by a variety of tactics. These may include redrawing precincts, moving polling locations, and changing the rules or dates for absentee or early voting.

South Carolina became the first state to require identification to vote, in 1950. Before 2000, only four other states joined South Carolina in requiring voter identification. In 2005, the Baker-Carter Commission recommended that all states move to requiring identification at the polls (National Conference of State Legislatures, 2016).

In 2000, only 14 states required any sort of voter-provided identification to cast a ballot. By 2012, 33 states had some form of mandatory voter identification provision. In just over a decade, the majority of states had shifted from not requiring identification to doing so (National Conference of State Legislatures, 2016).

Voter identification laws can take on two forms: strict and non-strict, as defined by the National Conference of State Legislatures. Non-strict identification laws allow prospective voters who lack proper identification to sign an affidavit or other form of statement and cast an unqualified ballot with no further action on their part. Strict identification laws require voters without identification to cast provisional ballots and provide adequate identification after the fact for their votes to count (National Conference of State Legislatures, 2016a).

The Kobach Factor

It would be nearly impossible to underestimate the importance of one person to the movement toward more restrictive voting. A Harvard-trained political scientist and attorney, Kansas-born and -raised Kris Kobach has become a national touchstone on the issue of illegal immigration. Kobach's crusade against undocumented immigrants produced a second area of focus for his agenda, the right to vote.

Kobach's rise to national prominence came after a long and troubled history in Kansas politics. A failed candidate for the U.S. House in 2002, Kobach became chairman of the Kansas Republican Party in 2007 and presided over a disastrous two-year tenure highlighted by Federal Election Commission violations and massive debt. A three-way primary in 2010 produced Kobach as the Republican Party's nominee for secretary of state, and he then won the general election. From that position he aggressively developed laws that would not only transform the franchise in Kansas but across the country (Horwitz, 2016).

Kobach's legal training provided him expertise in crafting legislation, and not only has he succeeded in passing voting restrictions in Kansas but in numerous other states across the country: notably, Arizona, Alabama, and Indiana (Hegeman, 2016). The spread of restrictive voting laws from Kansas to other states has drawn attention back to the source: Kobach. This attention has taken the form of heavy media publicity, scholarly attention, and numerous lawsuits. Kobach has lost most of these court cases, both in federal and in Kansas courts. For example, in the 2018 ruling *Fish v Kobach/Bednasek v Kobach* (decided together), Judge Julie Robinson ruled against Kobach and the proof-of-citizenship law he was defending, and even ordered the secretary of state to take continuing education courses in legal procedure. Later that year, Kobach barely won the Republican nomination for governor, only to be defeated by Democrat Laura Kelly in the general election. As this book goes to press, he is seeking the U.S. Senate seat being vacated by Pat Roberts in 2020.

Kobach's justification for supporting and implementing these restrictive laws has been that voter fraud is rampant in the United States, undermines democratic values, and is conducted primarily by the undocumented immigrants he also seeks stronger regulation to control (Eveld, 2016). Critics of Kobach claim that the small number of documented cases of voter fraud prior to his introduction of restrictive voting laws and the paucity of fraud convictions afterward suggest that the laws are meant to suppress voting (Editors, 2016).

Growth in Restrictive Laws

In 2000, no state had a strict version of the law that requires a photo identification in order to vote. Most states required no identification beyond a voter registration card. Not only has the majority of state law shifted to requiring some additional form of voter identification, but the most significant growth area has been in strict laws requiring photo ID. As of 2016, seven states mandated photo ID to vote and strictly limited which types of IDs would be allowed (generally requiring it to be state-issued, usually a driver's license for most voters). Three states had strict voter ID laws but the ID in question did not have to contain a photo. Nine states had laws allowing poll workers to request photo ID, but not to require it. Thirteen states had laws allowing poll workers to request, but not require ID, and this was not limited to photo IDs—these states allow utility bills with one's home address and name, for example, to be used as documentation. Finally, eighteen states do not have ID requirements for voting. These numbers are continually shifting due to court rulings (National Conference of State Legislatures, 2016a).

Kobach's presence as a leader in the movement would suggest that most states embracing the restrictive voter ID law would trend Republican. The voters most affected by voter ID restrictions are the youngest and those in the poorest social classes, who tend to vote Democratic. One criticism of the laws has been that they are a thinly veiled attempt to reduce Democratic vote totals (Keyes, 2016). As the wave of voter laws expanded, so did the types of state adding such laws. Alabama, the Dakotas, and Mississippi were in the vanguard of the restrictive law model in the early 2000s, but in 2005 solidly Democratic Washington State adopted a voting law statute, and swing states such as Pennsylvania and Virginia followed suit by 2012. Known for internecine politics that transcend partisanship, Democratic-leaning Rhode Island also passed a new ID law during this period. Thus, while the origins of restrictive voting laws can be traced to the GOP, they have at least been partially embraced by both parties, although in a much more pronounced way by Republicans, particularly those in "swing" or "battleground" states, plus Kansas. Furthermore, Democratic-leaning states also embraced a number of reforms meant to expand the franchise during this period, including voting by mail in Colorado, Oregon, and Washington, and automatic voter registration in Washington and California. Nearly all states also embraced early voting during this period, but despite boosters' optimistic predictions, the results of early voting on turnout have been disappointing (Stewart & Burden, 2014).

In 2018, voter approval of Amendment 4 reversing felony disenfranchisement in Florida was a dramatic variation from the pattern of increased voting restrictions in the battleground states, but only time will tell if this marks a reversal in course or an aberration.

Effects of the Restrictive Voting Law

Whether we are seeing a long-term political shift or a passing fad remains to be seen, but electoral laws have consequences. Even in the short term, they can impact elections, candidates, and policy. Do these laws have a suppressive effect on Democratic votes? Do they disproportionately affect younger citizens and racial minorities? Do they fight the voter fraud they are purported to defend against? What are the larger-scale effects on democracy that franchise restrictions impose?

In this book we have sought to answer the questions listed above. After situating these laws into a larger context of the four Mississippi Plans, subsequent chapters found that the photo ID laws have some surprising effects. Rather than suppressing votes, they appear to mobilize two different groups—African Americans, and Republicans. There is little evidence that they lower turnout, but they do appear to shift the electorate slightly to the GOP's benefit. Felony disenfranchisement produces a more direct and predicted result—a measurable shift toward a more Republican electorate, and a disproportionate number of African American voters disenfranchised. As for voter "caging," it is technically illegal as per the NVRA, but it still happens. The "stealth" nature of this process makes it maddeningly hard to quantify or assess, but we do know that it has been the subject of numerous court cases and political activism on the part of civil rights groups who oppose it. Finally, *gerrymandering* is a nebulous term. Drawing geographically compact districts does not necessarily enhance minority representation, and the United States's overall pattern of single-member districts and first-past-the-post elections tends to exaggerate the size of small majorities in most cases, regardless of whether legal protections against egregious gerrymandering are in place or not. All in all, the significant change in intent and scope of voter laws is a vitally important component of current-day American politics and one that calls for continued examination.

References

Bednasek v. Kobach 259 F. Supp. 3d 1193 (D. Kan. 2017).
Burden, B., & Stewart, C. III. (2014). *The measure of American elections*. Cambridge University Press.
Eveld, E. (2016). Kris Kobach defends prosecution of voter fraud cases in Kansas. *The Kansas City Star*. April 12.
Fish v. Kobach 189 F. Supp. 3d 1107 (D. Kan. 2016).
Hegeman, R. (2016). Timeline of Kris Kobach's drive to restrict voting in Kansas. *The Lawrence (KS) Journal World*. July 20.
Horwitz, S. (2016). The conservative gladiator from Kansas behind restrictive voting laws. *The Washington Post*. April 6.
Editors. *Kansas City Star*. (2016). Kris Kobach is a big fraud on Kansas voter fraud. May 15.
Keyes, S. (2016). Study finds Republican voter suppression is even more effective than you think. ThinkProgress.org. February 2.
National Conference of State Legislatures. (2016). History of voter ID.
National Conference of State Legislatures. (2016a). Voter identification requirements.

Afterword on the 2020 Election

Michael A. Smith

On Wednesday, January 6, 2021, a riotous mob seized the United States Capitol and held it for several hours, delaying the unsealing and certification of electoral votes until late that night and into the next morning. Shortly before the mob walked to the Capitol, they heard speeches from outgoing president Trump and his attorney Rudy Giuliani, in which their fears that the election had been stolen by massive electoral fraud were stoked. Trump said, "If you don't fight like hell you're not going to have a country anymore," and urged supporters to "walk down to the Capitol." Giuliani suggested "trial by combat." As this chapter goes to press, the death toll from that day stands at six, four Trump supporters and two capitol police officers. This was the first time the U.S. Capitol was seized since 1814.

How did this happen? What circumstances surrounding the election led to a riotous mob perpetuating this act of sedition after being stoked by the outgoing president?

Ironically, the 2020 United States presidential elections had been conducted with a remarkable degree of security. Led by Trump appointee Christopher Krebs, the United States Cybersecurity and Infrastructure Security Agency (CISA) called it "the most secure in American history" (CISA, 2020). CISA also maintained a Web and social media presence debunking false claims, including those made by the president himself. Trump fired Krebs via Twitter on November 17, 2020 (Collier et al., 2020).

The elections occurred during the worst pandemic to affect the United States since polio, as the rapidly spreading coronavirus that causes COVID-19 forced measures unheard of to most living Americans, including wearing protective masks in public, closing schools, restaurants, and bars, and discouraging public gatherings. The precautions varied from state to state and county to county, with Republican-voting "red" states and counties generally much more resistant to lockdowns and mask ordinances than were urban and Democratic areas (Goodkind, 2020).

Due to these precautions, states braced themselves for a record number of early ballots cast by mail. California, Washington, D.C., and Vermont sent a mail-in ballot to each registered voter for the first time, joining several states that had done so previously (Love, Stevens, & Gambio, 2020). Others, such as Kansas, expanded their existing early voting laws to allow any voter to request and cast an early ballot, either by mail or in an official ballot drop box, such as those used in other vote-by-mail states like Oregon and Colorado. Still others, such as Missouri, did not make these provisions, but they did pass laws allowing voters to cast absentee ballots without notarizing them if their reason for doing so was being at high risk for complications from COVID-19. For those who did vote in person, many took advantage of early voting. Election-day polling places were moved to larger spaces to accommodate social distancing. The table below summarizes state responses to the 2020 pandemic.

A number of states had regulations prohibiting county election workers from beginning to count the record number of mail-in ballots until the close of the polls on Election Day. In addition, several states allowed for ballots received within a certain "grace period" after the election to be counted, provided that the ballots were postmarked on or before Election Day. Yet other states required the ballots to be received, not counted by, Election Day. These variations among states included critical battleground states. For example, Pennsylvania law prohibited the counting of mail-in ballots until polls closed. The legacy news media announced repeatedly that not all ballots would be counted on Election Night, while state and county election workers urged patience. Both suggested that the election's winner would not be declared for several days (Wasserman, 2020).

Despite this, President Trump stated before the election that he expected the results of the election to be called on Election Night (Astor, 2020). Led by Trump himself, who had contracted and recovered from the virus along with the First Lady, Republicans tended to downplay the risks of COVID-19. Trump held several rallies at which most attendees were unmasked and no social distancing was practiced (Reichmann,

A.1. State Adjustments to the Coronavirus Pandemic 2020

States Mailing Ballots to All Registered Voters

California*	New Jersey*
Colorado	Oregon
District of Columbia*	Utah
Hawaii	Vermont*
Nevada*	Washington

*designates states doing this for the first time in 2020

Allowing No Excuse Absentee Voting

Delaware*
Massachusetts*
Missouri*

Other Changes to Ease Absentee Voting

Alaska	Nebraska
Arizona	North Carolina*
Florida	North Dakota
Georgia	Ohio
Idaho	Oklahoma*
Kansas	Pennsylvania*
Maine	Rhode Island*
Michigan*	South Dakota
Minnesota*	Virginia*
Montana*	Wyoming

Absentee Ballot Applications Mailed to All Registered Voters

Connecticut*	Maryland*
Delaware*	Massachusetts*
Illinois*	New Mexico*
Iowa*	Wisconsin*

Source: *New York Times*

Allowing COVID as a Reason to Vote Absentee

Alabama*	Kentucky*
Arkansas*	New Hampshire*
Connecticut*	West Virginia*

Excuse Required for Absentee Voting

Indiana	South Carolina**
Louisiana	Tennessee
Mississippi	Texas
New York	

**In South Carolina, an excuse was still required, but other changes were made to ease absentee voting.

2020). Former presidential candidate Herman Cain contracted COVID-19 and died after attending one such rally in Tulsa (Adams Wagner, 2020). Contradicting messages from his own campaign staff, Trump also urged his supporters to vote in person (Solender, 2020). Democrats and urban-area residents were more likely to vote by mail, while rural and Republican voters were more likely to vote in person on Election Day (Riccardi & Kastanis, 2020). For these reasons, it was anticipated that Trump might have appeared to be winning on Election Night and that his opponent Joe Biden's votes would accumulate as the mail-in ballots were counted in the ensuing days, particularly those from urban counties, creating a so-called "red mirage" (Wasserman). In fact, this is exactly what happened, as the battleground states of Michigan, Pennsylvania, Georgia, Arizona, and Nevada moved from the red to the blue column once all mail-in ballots were counted by the end of the week. Trump's senior advisor Jason Miller stoked the fears even more directly by warning beforehand that Democrats were plotting to "steal" the election (Rummler, 2020).

Election officials argued that the election was conducted with a remarkable degree of transparency and efficiency. Led by CISA, the federal and state governments and technology providers all put forth aggressive new computer security measures to prevent the election tampering that had been conducted by the Russian government and its proxies in 2016. CISA also warned that Iran and China might try to interfere (CISA, 2019). Approximately $350 million in grants from Facebook founder Mark Zuckerberg and his wife Priscilla Chan assisted localities in updating their voting equipment (Sheck, Hing, Robinson, & Stockton, 2020). William Evanina, director of the National Counterintelligence and Security Center, presented findings that the governments of China and Iran, as well as Russia, attempted to interfere in the 2020 election, either through falsely identified social media accounts or with actual attempts to infiltrate electronic voting machines (BBC, 2020). Both of these had occurred in 2016, but in 2020 the former—spreading false and/or toxic narratives on social media under false names—was far more widespread (Mueller, 2019).

What happened next is best described by a documented rhetorical strategy and logical fallacy called the *Gish gallop*. Named for a "young Earth" Biblical literalist who used the strategy himself, the Gish gallop is a strategy in which numerous false and unresearched but plausible-sounding allegations are rapid-fired against one's opponent, with the opponent challenged to disprove each one (Bokulich, 2013). These may be false, or they might be true facts stated out of context. Unlike the Scientific Method, the Gish gallop has nothing to do with establishing truth or falsity; rather, it is a psychological manipulation. For those who resort to it, the Gish gallop offers two rhetorical advantages. The first is that it creates an impression among observers that the allegations must be true because there are so many of them. Roughly summarized, the thinking is that while *all* of the allegations may not be true, with so many of them, surely at least *some* of them are. This has nothing to do with establishing objective truth or falsity, but it is a powerful tool for creating in observers' minds the idea that "where there's smoke, there's fire."

The second thing that makes the Gish gallop so insidious is that it puts the sparring partner in an impossible position. The party making the allegations need spend only a few minutes thinking up false but true-sounding allegations—no fact-checking is required. The other debater is put in an impossible position of having to carefully fact-check, research, and disprove (or corroborate, though that is rare) each allegation. This is impossible, because the false or out-of-context allegations can always be rapid-fired more quickly than each one can be thoroughly, rigorously fact-checked. The party using the Gish gallop wins by overwhelming their opponent, much like a computer virus that works by overwhelming the targeted system with too many requests for information.

Trump and his allies used the Gish gallop strategy to perfection during the election and aftermath. They fired off numerous lawsuits and other false allegations, including a widely believed but false allegation that voting machines sold by Dominion Voting Systems were "rigged" to favor Biden. This particular rumor circulated widely on the vast network of social media connections created for a conspiracy theory called QAnon, which in turn held that Democrats worshipped Satan and ran a child-trafficking ring (Collins, 2020). Two QAnon supporters, Reps. Marjorie Taylor Greene (R-Georgia) and Lauren Boebert (R-Colorado) were elected to the House in 2020 (Tulley-McManis, 2020).

The conspiracy theories and quickly-dismissed lawsuits fired off by Trump, Giuliani, and their supporters were extensive. What follows is a sampling.

- Allegations that Pennsylvania county election officials, particularly in Philadelphia, did not properly check signatures on absentee ballots. Similar allegations were made regarding Georgia.

- Allegations that ballots in Arizona marked with a Sharpie ™ brand marker were not read by the optical scanners

- Allegations that memory sticks containing voter data were not properly handled in Pennsylvania and Georgia

- Allegations that Michigan voting machines were "rigged" to switch votes from Donald Trump to Joe Biden

- Allegations that ballots were cast in the names of dead people in Michigan

- Allegations that Nevada officials reset the level of specificity required to electronically validate signatures to the lowest possible level

- A particularly bizarre allegation that the official numbers reported by counties to state election officials could not be accurate because the "leading numbers," or first digits in the sequences were different than what would be expected to occur due to a mathematical finding called Benford's Law (Reuters Staff, 2020).

The allegations went on and on, and because the Gish gallop was employed it would not be effective to repeat and rigorously fact-check each one here. Excellent sources compiled by reporters that do analyze many of the claims include Gerhart (2021), Woodward (2021), and Doran (2021). Like the CISA report, all of these analyses conclude that there was no widespread fraud in the 2020 presidential election, and that no valid objection based on the remaining technicalities could possibly have changed the outcome.

Trump supporters were unswayed by any of these arguments. Dismissing the legacy news media as hopelessly biased against their hero, they pressed onward with false claims, including those linked to conspiracy theories such as QAnon. In response, in January 2021, Dominion Voting Systems sued Giuliani, seeking $1.3 billion in damages (Polantz, 2021).

Starting later the same day as the Capitol rioting and lasting into the next morning, Congress certified the electoral votes. All Democrats and Independents voted to certify. Republicans were split. In the House, 138 Republicans voted to certify and 121 opposed. In the Senate, seven Republicans voted No on certification (Zhou, 2021). This represented a drop from the numbers of Republicans originally expected to object, which was estimated at 140 in the House and 14 in the Senate. Those switching from "no" to "yes" on certification are presumed to have done so in response to the Capitol rioting. President Biden was inaugurated on January 20 in a ceremony guarded by more than 20,000 National Guard troops (Zaiets et al., 2021). Almost immediately, the QAnon network began spreading a conspiracy theory that the inauguration was 'faked' (Link, 2021).

Dubbed the "Big Lie" by the legacy news media, Trump's Gish gallop won widespread support in the Republican Party, despite being factually baseless. An NPR/PBS NewsHour/Marist poll found that 60 percent of Americans trust the election results, but among Republicans that number dropped to one-quarter (Detro, Montenaro, & Davis, 2021). Senator Ben Sasse (R-Nebraska) told reporters that the vast majority of his Republican colleagues privately do not believe there was widespread election fraud. Instead, those objecting were trying to tap into the former president's electoral base. Sasse referred to these as "institutional arsonists" (Cheney, 2020).

This story continues to unfold as this book goes to press.

References

Adams Wagner, L. J. (2020). Former GOP presidential hopeful Herman Cain dies of COVID-19. Associated Press. July 30.

Astor, M. (2020). We have never had final results on Election Day. *New York Times*. November 1.

BBC News Service. (2020). U.S. election 2020: China, Russia, and Iran "trying to influence" the vote. August 8.

Bokulich, P. (2013). Gish gallop (fallacy of the day). *(Pseudo-)Science Blog*. November 18.

Collier, K., Tur, K., Ainsley, J., & Dilanian, K. (2020). Trump fires head of election cybersecurity who debunked conspiracy theories. *NBC News*. November 17.

Collins, B. (2020). QAnon's Dominion voter fraud conspiracy reaches the president. *NBC News*. November 13.

Detrow, S., Montenaro, D., & Davis, S. Most Americans believe the election results—Some don't. NPR. December 9.

Doran, W. (2021). Fact check: NC's Madison Cawthorn explains challenge to Biden's win. Here's what he got wrong. *Raleigh News & Observer*. January 4 (Updated January 6).

Cheney, K. "Institutional arsonist members of Congress": Sasse rips GOP lawmakers challenging 2020 results. *Politico*. December 31.

Gerhart, A. (2021). Election results under attack: Here are the facts. *Washington Post*. January 14.

Goodkind, N. (2020). States with the least coronavirus restrictions all voted for Trump. *Fortune*. May 22.

Link, D. (2021). Fact check: No basis for claims that President Joe Biden's inauguration was faked. *USA Today*. January 28.

Love, J., Stevens, M., & Gamio, L. (2020). Where Americans can vote by mail in the 2020 elections. *New York Times*. August 14.

Mueller, R. S. III. (2019). Report on the investigation into Russian interference in the 2016 election. U.S. Department of Justice.

Poleantz, K. (2021). Election technology company Dominion sues Giuliani for $1.3 billion over "Big Lie" about election fraud. CNN. January 25.

Reichmann, D. (2020). As virus surges, Trump rallies keep packing in thousands. AP. October 29.

Reuters Staff. (2020). Fact check: Deviation from Benford's Law does not prove election fraud. November 10.

Riccardi, N., & Kastanis, A. (2020). Trump's Election Day surge powered by small-town America. AP. November 4.

Rummler, O. (2020). Trump advisor falsely claims that Democrats could "steal" electoral votes. *Axios*. November 1.

Scheck, T., Hing, G., Robinson, S., & Stockton, G. How private money from Facebook's CEO saved the election. National Public Radio. December 8.

Solender, A. (2020). Trump votes in person and slams mail-in voting as campaign urges voters to vote by mail. *Forbes*. October 24.

Tulley-McManus, K. QAnon goes to Washington: Two supporters win seats in Congress. *Roll Call*. November 5.

United States Cybersecurity and Infrastructure Security Agency (CISA). (2019). Joint statement from the DOJ, DOD, DJS, DNI, FBI, NSA, and CISA on ensuring security of the 2020 elections. November 5. Revised January 21, 2021.

United States Cybersecurity and Infrastructure Security Agency (CISA). (2020). Joint statement from Election Infrastructure Government Coordinating Council & the Election Infrastructure Sector Coordinating Executive Committee." November 12.

Wasserman, D. (2020). Beware the "blue mirage" and "red mirage" on election night. *NBC News*. November 3.

Woodward, C. (2021). AP fact check: Trump's false claims fuel on a day of chaos. AP. January 6.

Zaiets, K., Zarracina, J., & Hjelmgaard, K. (2021). Inauguration threats: Over 20,000 National Guard troops to provide security against inauguration threats in Washington." *USA Today*. January 14.

Zhou, L. (2021). 147 Republican lawmakers still objected to the election results after the Capitol attack. *Vox.* January 7.

Contributors

Kevin Anderson is Professor of Political Science at Eastern Illinois University. He teaches courses in American government, Political Theory, and African American politics. His first book *Agitations: Ideologies and Strategies in African American Politics* (University of Arkansas Press, 2010), explores the evolution of political ideology within African American politics. His second book is a co-authored work, *State Voting Laws in America: Historical Statutes and Their Modern Implications* (Palgrave Pivot, 2015) with Professors Michael A. Smith of Emporia State University and Chapman Rackaway (listed below). This book explores the history, theories, and evolving politics surrounding the right to vote in American politics.

Russell Brooker is Professor of Political Science at Alverno College in Milwaukee, Wisconsin. He teaches courses in political science, sociology, statistics, and African American history. He received his Ph.D. in Political Science from the University of Chicago in 1981. He has written two books. He co-authored *Public Opinion in the Twenty-First Century: Let the People Speak?* in 2006. In 2016, he wrote *The American Civil Rights Movement 1865–1950: Black Agency and People of Good Will*. He has recently written a chapter in *Civil Liberties in Real Life* on African Americans during the Jim Crow era. He is on the board of directors of America's Black Holocaust Museum and has written several displays for the organization's website, abhmuseum.org. He was a Fulbright Scholar in 2006 in Vietnam and has taught three semesters in Ho Chi Minh City.

Deborah G. Hann is an Assistant Professor at Emporia State University in Emporia, Kansas. After receiving her Ph.D. from the Geography

Department at Texas State University, she has continued her research examining the geographic content inherent within material culture such as children's literature and cookbooks. Her research particularly focuses upon how that content conveys narratives of places and peoples, as well as how material culture contributes to mental maps and identities. She teaches Cartography, Cultural Geography, and more concentrated classes like the World in Film, and Food, Culture, and Place.

Brian Hollenbeck is a Professor of Mathematics and the chair of the Department of Mathematics and Economics at Emporia State University. He is currently the National President of Kappa Mu Epsilon, Mathematics Honor Society. He received his Ph.D. from the University of Missouri. His research interests include harmonic analysis and complex analysis, mathematical modeling, and innovation in teaching.

Chapman Rackaway is a Professor and Chairperson of Political Science at Radford University. Dr. Rackaway's teaching and scholarly interests focus on the intersection of republican democracy and professional electioneering. He teaches classes in Political Parties, Political Campaign Management, Interest Groups and Lobbying, and Campaign Finance. He is the author of *Civic Failure and its Threat to American Democracy: Operator Error* (Lexington Press 2016) co-editor of *Parties Under Pressure* (Palgrave 2017) and *The Unorthodox Presidency of Donald Trump*, as well as other books on American politics, political communication, and voting behavior. His professional portfolio can be found at www.chapmanrackaway.com.

Bekah Selby earned her Ph.D. in Economics from the University of Oregon, and then became an Assistant Professor of Economics at Emporia State University and is the Associate Director for Community Research. At ESU, she developed both the Master of Science in Informatics - Quantitative Economics concentration along with a similar graduate certificate program. Bekah serves in a wide array of leadership roles including the steering committee of the national American Democracy Project, Lyon County Food and Farm Council, Healthier Lyon County, and many others. She is an active scholar, especially in applied econometrics and research related to civic engagement.

Michael A. Smith is Professor of Political Science and Chair of Social Sciences, Sociology, and Criminology at Emporia State University. Dr.

Smith studies state and local government, campaigns and elections, and political philosophy. His latest book prior to this one is *Low Taxes and Small Government: Sam Brownback's Great Experiment in Kansas* (2019, with Robert J. Grover and Rob Catlett). He was also an expert witness in *Bednasek v. Kobach*. Dr. Smith earned his doctorate from The University of Missouri.

Linda M. Trautman is a tenured Associate Professor of Political Science at Ohio University-Lancaster. She has taught at Ohio University since 2005. Prior to teaching at Ohio University, she was a faculty member at Wellesley College in Boston, MA. Her areas of expertise in American politics include national and state legislative politics, voting behavior, race and ethnic politics, and urban governance. Dr. Trautman has published works on the politics of partisan representation in American voting and the dynamics of racial advocacy and bill sponsorship in state legislatures. She has also been involved in voting rights and social justice initiatives through the Southern Leadership for Voter Engagement organization. She completed her Ph.D. at The Ohio State University with a specialization in American Politics.

Ryan E. Voris is an assistant professor of political science in the Department of History and Political Science at Abraham Baldwin Agricultural College. His research focuses primarily on how voter identification laws impact voting in the United States, including the impact of these laws on voter turnout and ballot access. Other research examines gubernatorial campaign stops in the 2018 elections. He received his doctorate from the University of Kentucky.

Index

Absentee voting, 35, 45, 57, 60, 61, 159, 166–67, 169
African-American voter turnout. See election turnout
Annexation, 31
At large voting, 5, 29–31
Australian ballot, 19

Backlash effect, 2–4, 5, 7, 34, 47, 62–63, 68, 71–86, 111
Ballot boxes, 24, 35, 145
Biden, Joseph, 168–71
Black voter turnout. See voter turnout
"Bleached" districts. 33

CISA. See United States Cybersecurity and Infrastructure Security Agency
Civil Rights Act (1964), 28, 143
Civil Rights Movement, 10, 21, 24, 28, 40, 45, 56, 68, 112
Clinton, Hillary, 49, 75, 88
Colfax, Louisiana, 15, 143
Commission on Federal Election Reform, 49–50, 52. See also photo ID
Congress of Racial Equality (CORE), 24
Conspiracy theories, 169–71

Convex hull, 129–30
Coronavirus. See COVID-19
County unit system (Georgia), 23
COVID-19, 166–68
Cracking. See districts, drawing of

Department of Justice (DOJ). See United States Department of Justice
Department of Motor Vehicles (DMV), 3. See also National Voter Registration Act of 1993
Districts, drawing of. See also gerrymandering
  and compactness, 129–31, 133–34, 141
  and "cracking and packing," 29, 32–33, 131, 133
  and efficiency gap, 132–34
  and fairness, 109, 121, 135, 140
  and simulation, 134–36, 139–40
Du Bois, W. E. B., 13, 16–17, 40–41, 146–47, 156

Early voting, 36, 45, 58, 74, 77–81, 88–89, 151, 159, 162, 166
Edmund Pettus Bridge, 25, 120, 133
Efficiency gap. See districts, drawing of

179

Election reform, 2, 10, 19, 41, 45–50, 52, 57, 66, 68, 110–13, 115–16, 121–23, 145, 149–50, 154–55
Election turnout, 4–7, 34, 45–47, 49, 51, 53, 55–63, 65–70, 73–77, 79, 82–84, 87, 90–92, 94, 98, 102–107, 109–10, 113–14, 116–18, 120, 121, 123, 136, 141, 156–58, 162, 177
Election violence 2, 9, 13–14, 16–17, 20. *See also* voter intimidation

Federal Elections "Force" Bill, 15
Felony disenfranchisement, 4–7, 77–79, 81, 109–24, 149, 162

Gerrymandering 4, 6–7, 29, 34, 38, 41–42, 125–31, 133, 135–36, 139–41, 149
Gish gallop, 168–71
Giuliani, Rudolph, 165, 169, 170
Golden Week. *See* Souls to the Polls
"Good character" test, 17–18, 149
Grandfather clause, 12, 18, 21, 146–49

Help America Vote Act (HAVA), 46, 49, 149

Johnson, Lyndon, 25, 41

Kobach, Kris, 1, 3, 8, 76, 89–90, 94, 160–61
Krebs, Christopher. *See* United States Cybersecurity and Infrastructure Security Agency

Literacy test, 2, 14, 17–18, 21, 23, 26, 109, 146–47
Lodge, Henry Cabot, 15

Mail. *See* voting by mail
Mississippi Plans, 10–38
  First Mississippi Plan, 13–15
  Second Mississippi Plan, 16–21
  Third Mississippi Plan, 29–34
  Fourth Mississippi Plan, 34–38
Moral turpitude, 18
Motor voter. *See* National Voter Registration Act of 1993
Multi-member districts, 30

National Association for the Advancement of Colored People (NAACP), 17, 20–22, 24, 30, 34, 40, 42, 65, 67, 69, 74, 146–47, 150–51, 155–57
National Voter Registration Act of 1993, 3–4, 57, 83, 90, 157
Numbered post system, 40

Obama, Barack, 73, 76, 80–81, 88, 151

Packing. *See* districts, drawing of
Pandemic. *See* COVID-19
Partisan vote share, 109
Photo ID laws, 3–4, 45–70, 90, 162
  and African Americans, 56, 57–58, 61
  concerns over access, 46–47, 50–51, 54–55, 67
  confidence in elections, 50
  costs to voting, 52, 55, 57–58, 65
  effects on turnout, 54–55, 59–63, 67–68
  Indiana Photo ID Law, 50
  laws in effect 2016, 53–54
  legal challenges, 52, 55, 63–66
  mobilization effects, 56, 62–63
  NCSL classification of, 54
  partisan adoption of, 46, 52–53, 66–67

public support for, 46
spread of, 47–49
state constitutions, 64–65
state courts, 64–66
Pig law, 14, 35
Policy reform, 112, 122. *See also* election reform
Polygon, 23, 129, 130
Poll tax, 2, 14–15, 17–18, 21, 23, 28, 38, 51, 58, 109, 145–48, 150
Preclearance, 26, 31–32, 38, 121, 145
Proof-of-citizenship laws, 1, 3–4, 34, 37, 89–91, 94–102, 159
Proportional representation, 6, 140

Qanon. *See* conspiracy theories
Qualifications. *See* voting qualifications

Reconstructions, 10–28
   First Reconstruction, 12–13
   Second Reconstruction, 24–28
Reform. *See* election reform, policy reform
Residency requirements, 19
Romney, Willard Mitt, 4, 71, 75, 80, 82
Runoff elections, 30–31

Selma, Alabama, 25
Simulation. *See* districts, drawing of
Souls to the Polls, 36, 74, 88
Southern Christian Leadership Conference (SCLC), 24
Student Nonviolent Coordinating Committee (SNCC), 24

Trump, Donald, 39, 75, 88, 136, 153, 165–66, 168–71
Turnout. *See* election turnout

Understanding clauses, 17–18
United States Cybersecurity and Infrastructure Security Agency (CISA), 165, 168, 170
United States Department of Justice, 10, 22, 26, 28, 32

Voter caging, 3–4, 6, 148–49, 159, 162. *See also* voter purges
Vote denial, 23, 25, 29, 31–32, 34, 38
Vote dilution, 9–10, 23–25, 28–29, 31–32, 34, 38, 110
Voter fraud, 3, 7, 11, 37, 46, 48, 50–52, 54, 64–65, 87, 90, 148, 152, 161–62
   perceptions of, 46
   presence in elections, 48, 55, 67
Voter Education Project, 24
Voter identification. *See* Photo ID laws
Voter intimidation, 9, 16, 20
Voter purges, 35. *See also* voter caging
Voting qualifications, 10, 18–19, 26, 65
Voting reforms, 10. *See also* policy reforms
Voter suppression. *See* voter intimidation, voter purges
Voter turnout. *See* election turnout
Voting by mail, 57, 60, 89, 148–49, 162, 166–68
Voting Rights Act (1965), 2–3, 10, 21, 24–27, 31, 38–39, 109, 121, 145, 151–52

Wasted vote(s), 132
White primary, 19, 21, 151
Wilmington, North Carolina, 14

Court Cases

Allen v. State Board of Elections 393 US 344 (1969), 28
Baker v. Carr 369 US 186 (1962), 23, 38
Bednasek v. Kobach. *See* Fish v. Kobach
Benisek v. Lamone 585 US (2018), 38
City of Mobile v. Bolden 446 US 55 (1980), 31
Crawford v. Marion County Election Board 553 US 181 (2008), 3, 37, 50–53, 64, 66, 67–68, 83, 88, 197, 156
Ex parte Yarbrough 110 US 651 (1884), 15
Fish v. Kobach D. Kan (2016), 160, 163
Giles v. Harris 189 US 475 (1903), 21
Gomillion v. Lightfoot 344 US 339 (1960), 23
Gray v. Sanders 372 US 368 (1963), 33
Grovey v. Townsend 295 US 45 (1935), 22
Guinn v. United States 238 US 347 (1915), 21
Harper v. Virginia Board of Elections 383 US 663 (1966), 28
James v. Bowman 190 US 127 (1903), 21
Katzenbach v. Morgan 384 US 641 (1966), 28
Lamone v. Benisek 588 US (2019), 38
Nixon v. Condon 286 US 73 (1932), 22
Nixon v. Herndon 273 US 536 (1927), 21
Reynolds v. Sims 377 US 533 (1964), 24, 147, 157
Rucho v. Common Cause 585 US (2019), 38, 125, 127, 131, 134, 136, 139–41
Shaw v. Hunt 517 US 899 (1996), 33
Shaw v. Reno 509 US 630 (1993), 33
Shelby County v. Holder 570 US 529 (2013), 33, 38, 41, 84, 121, 123, 145, 157
Smith v. Allwright 321 US 649 (1944), 22, 25, 151
Thornburg v. Gingles 478 US 30 (1986), 32
US v. Classic 313 US 299 (1941), 22, 147, 158
Wesberry v. Sanders 376 US 1 (1964), 24
Williams v. Mississippi 170 US 213 (1898), 21

www.ingramcontent.com/pod-product-compliance
Ingram Content Group UK Ltd.
Pitfield, Milton Keynes, MK11 3LW, UK
UKHW042013140426
5217IPUK00015B/1151